TOP C-TURVY

An Olla Podrida of
OPERA ANECDOTES

GERRY ZWIRN

authorHOUSE®

AuthorHouse™ UK
1663 Liberty Drive
Bloomington, IN 47403 USA
www.authorhouse.co.uk
Phone: 0800 047 8203 (Domestic TFN)
+44 1908 723714 (International)

Published by AuthorHouse 06/03/2019

ISBN: 978-1-7283-8779-6 (sc)
ISBN: 978-1-7283-8780-2 (e)

Print information available on the last page.

Aïda

Ask any opera lover the name of the Verdi opera performed at the opening of the new Cairo Opera House and the answer is sure to be *Aïda*. But it wasn't *Aïda;* it was *Rigoletto*. It should have been *Aïda* but due to the outbreak of the Franco-Prussian War the scenery and costumes were holed up in Paris and couldn't be shipped out, so *Rigoletto* was performed instead. That was in November 1869.

Aïda eventually had its world premiere in Cairo on 24 December 1871. It was *not* conducted by Verdi, as is often stated, but by Giovanni Bottesini, the famous double-bass player and composer; Verdi conducted it at La Scala six weeks later. It was an overwhelming success and has since become one of the three most performed operas in the world.

But a certain Prospero Bertani felt very differently about it. He had travelled twice from Reggio Emilia to Parma to hear the new opera and disliked it so much that he wrote to Verdi demanding his money back! Here's his letter. [Author's translation]

On the second of this month I went to Parma to hear your opera, *Aïda*. I didn't like it. On the train home I listened to the opinions of my fellow travellers, most of whom agreed *Aïda* was a wonderful opera. Two nights later I returned to Parma but after the performance I reached the same conclusion: the opera contains nothing thrilling or electrifying, and if it weren't for the scenery no one would sit through it. This opera, after a few performances, will just gather dust in the archives.

Dear maestro, to go and hear your opera twice has cost me lire 31.80, made up as follows:

one way fare……………………..lire		2.60
return fare		3.30
theatre		8.00
disgusting dinner at the station		<u>2.00</u>
		15.90
multiplied by 2		31.80

I am from a poor family and this 31.80 is for me an irreparable loss that haunts me like a spectre. I am therefore requesting that you refund me the above amount.

Verdi, highly amused, instructed his publisher Ricordi to reimburse the haunted Bertani, but to deduct four lire for the two 'disgusting dinners' which, as Verdi pointed out, he could have eaten at home.

Reposing in the archives of the New York Met is a letter from the wife of an American millionaire, a boxholder in the fabled Diamond Horseshoe. In it she asks whether the management would be kind enough to postpone the famous tenor aria 'Celeste Aida', which, she was told, comes almost at the beginning of the opera, to later in the act because she could not possibly arrive in time to hear Jean de Reszke sing it and still be 'fashionably late'.

Barber of Seville

Opera buffs may be amused to learn that in earlier times, the so-called Lesson Scene in the *Barber of Seville* was used by the reigning prima donna for a mini-concert, much to the delight of her adoring fans. Although Rossini composed music for this scene, it was omitted by most Rosinas, who sang instead their own favourites. Thus Patti, Melba, Tetrazzini, Sembrich, Galli-Curci and other fashionable songbirds thought nothing of interpolating such showpieces as 'Lo, here the gentle lark', 'Home, sweet home', 'Il bacio', Tosti's 'Serenata', 'L'éclat de rire,' 'Les filles de Cadiz', 'Ombre legère', ' Mercè dilette amiche', 'Der Hölle Rache', Strauss' 'Frühlingstimmen', 'The Carnival of Venice' or the Mad Scenes from *Lucia di Lammermoor* and *Hamlet*. The fact that none of these pieces were composed by Rossini was of no importance; the public came to hear Patti, Melba etc, not Rossini.

This practice continued well into the 20th century, until Conchita Supervia, during the Rossini revival of the mid-1920s, restored the music to its rightful place, at the same time restoring the role of Rosina to mezzo-soprano.

It's also not generally known that Rossini composed an aria for Rosina in act 2 but it's not part of the score. 'Ah, se è ver in tal momento' was sung at the first London performance of the opera in 1818 by the French soprano Joséphine Fodor-Mainvielle. It had not been heard since, nor ever recorded, until it was introduced into the 2005 Madrid production of *The*

Barber, when it was sung by Maria Bayo. It may be heard in the DVD of that performance.

As for Almaviva's final aria 'Il più lieto, il più felice', this was considered too difficult for most tenors to sing and so was omitted; Rossini subsequently used it as the rondo finale for *La Cenerentola,* where it became 'Non più mesta.' After an absence of about 150 years it re-appeared at a Met Opera production in the 1950s, when it was sung by Cesare Valletti; more recently tenors such as Juan Diego Florez and William Matteuzzi have restored it.

Beecham, Sir Thomas

Britain's most colourful and enigmatic conductor was undoubtedly Sir Thomas Beecham (1879-1961). In addition to some brilliant recordings, he left behind a wealth of spicy stories, jokes and anecdotes some of which regretfully cannot be reprinted here. However, the following may offer some compensation.

During auditions in Paris for Beecham's recording of *Carmen,* a certain baritone bellowed his way at full voice through the Toreador Song. After he had finished Sir Thomas turned to his assistant and said "This fellow thinks *he's* the bloody bull!"

While rehearsing the last act of *La bohème* Beecham couldn't hear the dying Mimi as she lay stretched out on her bed. "More voice, please", he asked. "I'm sorry', protested the soprano, "but I can't give of my best in this position". "Well, madam", Sir Thomas replied, thoughtfully stroking his beard, "I would have thought any woman would give of her best in *that* position!"

The horse in *Cavalleria Rusticana,* what with the loud cracking of Alfio's whip and other stage noises, was becoming restless, until he could bear no more and Nature intervened. Sir Thomas, with a mischievous twinkle in his eye, turned to the audience and said;" My humble apologies, but gad, what a critic!"

During a rehearsal of *Salome* at Covent Garden John the Baptist failed to appear on cue. Putting down his baton Sir Thomas demanded, "Where is the prophet?" When someone asked him later whether he was referring to the character on stage or to the financial situation of the company, he replied "*Both!*"

Rehearsals for Massenet's *Don Quixote* were not going well. In the death scene in act 5 the Dulcinée, sung by Sadoven, complained that Chaliapin as Don Quixote always died too soon. Replied Sir Thomas: "Madam, you are gravely in error; no opera star has yet died soon enough for me!"

Bizet and Carmen

Operatic legend dies hard. *Failure, fiasco* and *flop* are some of the terms still bandied about by uninformed writers when describing the premiere of *Carmen*. Furthermore, many biographers still perpetuate the myth that Bizet, following the 'failure' of *Carmen*, died of a broken heart, aged 36.

The facts speak differently. First given at the Opéra-Comique on 3 March 1875, *Carmen* ran for 35 performances during the remainder of the season. Hardly a 'failure', even if the theatre was never more than half-full at most performances and that the box-office takings were insufficient to cover the costs of production.

As for Bizet dying of a 'broken heart', a weak heart is nearer the truth. Never of a strong constitution, he had imprudently gone swimming in cold river-water some weeks before, bringing on severe rheumatism leading to partial paralysis and heart failure. For a full account of his last days see *Bizet and his World* by Mina Curtiss (Secker & Warburg 1959) who based her book on a collection of previously unpublished material that came into her possession in the 1950s.

What is it about the role of Carmen that attracts so many singers? Almost every female singer of note, whether soprano, mezzo or contralto has, at one time or other in her career, been tempted to sing Bizet's enigmatic gypsy. The roster of great names is indeed impressive. First was Célestine

Galli-Marié, who sang the authentic Opéra-Comique version, that is, with spoken dialogue. After Galli-Marié came, in chronological order, Pauline Lucca, Emma Calvé, Zélie de Lussan, Minnie Hauk, Geraldine Farrar, Maria Gay, Mary Garden, Conchita Supervia, Maria Jeritza and Rosa Ponselle, to name a few. A later generation saw Jane Rhodes, Giulietta Simionato, Risë Stevens, Regina Resnik, Joyce Blackham and Marilyn Horne, all mezzos. On record, the part has been sung, *inter alia,* by Victoria de los Angeles, Leontyne Price, Christa Ludwig and Maria Callas. Indeed, at the time of writing, over 30 different complete recordings of *Carmen* have been issued, and this figure does not include pirated versions.

Of the various highlight recordings, the one featuring Geraldine Farrar deserves special mention. She not only had the voice, the temperament, the personality and the looks: she was also the first Carmen slim enough to be convincing onstage. Before her, other interpreters, however gifted vocally, tended to be 'generously endowed'; today, they would be laughed off the stage. Farrar's interpretation of the 'Seguidilla' was years ahead of its time (it was recorded in 1914). The way she laughs on the words 'Mon amoureux, il est au diable' and the sheer suggestiveness of 'Mon pauvre coeur très consolable', as she flirts with Don José, are magical.

Although the role is not demanding vocally, Carmen, like Madame Butterfly, is virtually onstage the whole time, from her dramatic entrance in act 1, usually with hand on hip and flower in mouth, to her violent death in act 4. But whatever our opinion of her, Carmen is no slut, and any attempt to portray her as such, as has been seen in some modern productions, is to be vigorously condemned.

While on the subject of correcting errors about *Carmen,* Ernest Newman, doyen of English music critics, made a careless gaffe in his *More Opera Nights* when he mistranslated Don José's lowly rank of *brigadier* (corporal) as 'brigadier', which is even higher than a colonel! Another, more common error is the 'rose' that Carmen throws at Don José in act 1: it was a cassia-flower, not a rose.

A contentious issue in *Carmen* is the high B flat sung by Don José in the phrase 'Et j'étais une chose a toi!' near the end of his Flower Song. Bizet marked it to be sung *pianissimo*, a marking which Newman called 'a technical blunder', and indeed most tenors, either on stage or on record, opt for a *fortissimo*. Nicolai Gedda, who sang the role many times and who recorded it twice– I myself heard him at La Scala – when making the complete recording with Callas, sang three versions of the phrase: *pianissimo, mezzo-forte and fortissimo*. "Make your choice!" he told the sound engineers at the time: they chose *mezzo-forte*, which certainly sounds more convincing than the seldom recorded *pianissimo* version which, to my ears, sounds psychologically wrong.

Finally, it's not generally known that Bizet, in addition to his gifts as a composer, was a pianist of exceptional talent blessed with a phenomenal memory, as illustrated by the following anecdote.

One evening he attended a soirée at Fromenthal Halévy's house in Paris, at which Franz Liszt was the guest of honour. Liszt had performed a new and fiendishly difficult composition of his own, declaring that he knew only two pianists capable of playing it: Hans von Bülow and himself. At Halévy's suggestion, Bizet then sat at the piano and played a passage from the work from memory. Liszt, completely amazed, then produced the manuscript and Bizet played the piece perfectly without any mistakes, to the astonishment of everyone present.

When he had finished, Liszt said: "I had thought that there were only two men capable of surmounting the difficulties with which I ornamented this piece. I was wrong: there are three of us, and to be fair I should add that the youngest is perhaps the boldest and the most brilliant". Bizet at the time was only 23!

La bohème

How many opera lovers know that the celebrated quartet that closes the third act of *La bohème* was originally a song composed by Puccini some eight years earlier? Titled 'Sole e Amore', it can be heard on a recital of Puccini songs recorded by the Italo-American soprano Marcella Reale.

Nor is this the only self-borrowing in the opera. Musetta's popular waltz song, 'Quando m'en vo' soletta', sung to death by practically every aspiring lyric soprano, was Puccini's offering for the launching of a battleship in the dockyards of Genoa!

'Vecchia zimarra', the famous bass aria sung by Colline in act 4 as he bids farewell to his well-worn coat, was on one notable occasion sung by a tenor; his name was Caruso.

During a performance of the opera in Philadelphia Andres de Segurola, the bass singing Colline, discovered he was losing his voice. By the time act 4 came he was practically hoarse and could sing no more, whereupon Caruso offered to sing the aria for him. Turning his back to the audience Caruso sang it in the original key, while de Segurola mimed the words. Apart from the conductor, no one in the theatre was aware that it was Caruso and de Segurola received the customary applause. Although Caruso was persuaded to record the aria he refused permission for it to be published, but in 1948 it was issued on a 78 rpm and later on LP and CD Caruso collections.

Puccini's opera is not the only one to be based on Henri Mürger's novel. Ruggero Leoncavallo, composer of *I Pagliacci,* also wrote an opera on the same subject, sparking off a bitter feud between the two composers that was never really healed.

In 1894, after the success of *Manon Lescaut,* Puccini was in Milan's Galleria when he met by chance Leoncavallo. During the conversation, which naturally turned to opera, Puccini casually remarked that his next work was to be based on Murger's novel (about a year earlier Leoncavallo, who wrote his own libretti, had sent Puccini a scenario of *La bohème* but Puccini had rejected it as being unsuitable). In a furious rage Leoncavallo jumped up from his chair and accused Puccini of stealing his idea, as he himself was engaged in writing a *La bohème*. "In that case', Puccini calmly replied, "there will be two *Bohèmes*".

The next morning the Milan morning newspaper *Il Secolo* announced that the celebrated composer Ruggero Leoncavallo was composing an opera to be called *La bohème*. A few hours later the *Corriere della Sera,* an afternoon newspaper, announced that the celebrated composer Giacomo Puccini was composing an opera to be called *La bohème;* the race was on.

Puccini's opera was produced in 1896, Leoncavallo's in 1897. But from the start it was obvious that Puccini's would emerge the winner while Leoncavallo's was an also-ran. Within a few months Puccini's opera was sweeping the world; Leoncavallo's, after its first performance, has seldom been given.

At a performance of *La bohème* at Covent Garden in the 1930s, Beniamino Gigli proved himself an accomplished fireman as well as an accomplished tenor. As he was singing 'Che gelida manina' he noticed that the little pot-bellied stove used by the Bohemians to keep warm had caught fire. Still singing, he grabbed the bottle of water used to revive the fainting Mimi and emptied its contents onto the fire inside the stove, but to no avail. Walking quickly to the wings, and in time to the music, he sang "Please fire, please fire, please fire'. Someone got the message and handed him a jug of water but it too was of no use. By this time Mimi had begun her aria. Nothing daunted, Gigli returned to the wings and, on being handed a bucket of water, succeeded in quenching the flames.

While we can't be sure that Gigli's prompt action saved Covent Garden from a fire as devastating as that which caused it to burn down in 1856, he received recognition for his firefighting skills the next morning when the *Daily Herald* published a headline that read:

AT COVENT GARDEN LAST NIGHT

GIGLI PUT FIRE INTO LA BOHEME!

Fictitious as the episodes may be in *La bohème*, there was nothing fictitious about the four members of the garret. All four, immortalised in Mürger's novel, existed in real life, as did Mimi and Musetta, albeit under different names.

Rodolfo the poet was Henri Mürger himself. He was a struggling young writer at the time and knew what day-to-day living was all about. Marcello was made up of two of Mürger's friends, Tabar and Lazare, both of whom were painters. Schaunard, in real life, was Alexandre Schanne, musician and painter. Colline the philosopher was, like Marcello, made up of two people, Wallon and Trapadoux. Wallon wore a shabby old coat the pockets of which were stuffed with books: the coat became the inspiration for 'Vecchia zimara' mentioned above.

Mimi, it seems, was a composite of two girls, one of whom was named Lucille – hence Mimi's opening words 'They call me Mimi but my name is Lucia". Musetta in real life was Marie Roux, a well-known artist's model whose likeness may be seen in several paintings by Ingres. After saving up enough money Marie left Paris in 1863 and made her way to Marseille, where she boarded a ship bound for Algiers. This was the ill-fated *Atlas* which went down in the Mediterranean taking passengers and crew with her.

Maria Callas

No opera singer, either alive or dead, made such an impact on the world of opera, or has been the subject of so much adulation and controversy, as Maria Callas. Over 30 full-length biographies, not to mention countless articles, have been written about the Greek diva. She was also the subject of two stage plays, *The Lisbon Traviata* and *Master Class*, as well as the films *Callas Forever* directed by Franco Zeffirelli. and *Maria, by Callas*. Her recordings of such operas as *Tosca, Lucia, Norma, Traviata, Medea* and *Anna Bolena* still remain, after 50 years, proof of her inimitable artistry, vocal technique and powers of interpretation. Her influence was so great that after her death in 1977 people spoke of BC, 'before Callas' and 'AD', after Callas.

During her relatively short career Callas was at the centre of several well-publicized scandals and litigations, providing a rich fund of anecdotes for her fans and detractors. Here are a few, with their relevant dates, taken at random.

Verona 1947

Maria Callas made her Italian debut on 3 August at the Arena di Verona in *La Gioconda,* an event arousing little interest. Her big break came in 1949 in Venice when she was appearing in *Die Walküre.* The soprano engaged for the role of Elvira in *I Puritani* fell ill and Callas was asked to take over the part. Although she had never sung Elvira before she learnt it in the six days preceding the opening night while continuing to sing in *Die Walküre.* To sing Brünnhilde one night and Elvira the next was a first in opera history, which is when the name of Maria Callas first made international headlines.

Milan 1953

This was when Callas began to astonish the world with her miraculous weight loss. In a matter of a few months she shed about 20 kilos, apparently with little effort. How was it done? Because she refused to disclose details we have to turn to her husband's biography, *My wife Maria Callas,* for an account of what happened.

Meneghini relates that one evening, when he was at La Scala, an usher came to his seat and told him that his wife had phoned urgently and that he must return immediately to their hotel room. As he entered it he was greeted with the words "Battista, I killed it!" She then went on to explain that while she was having her bath she had removed a long section of tapeworm which she had killed. Their doctor had told them that the tapeworm must be removed completely, for which he prescribed some medicine. Two days later Callas had rid herself completely of it.

During the next few weeks, Callas sensed that 'something within her was changing at a startling rate'; in one week, Meneghini relates, she lost about three kilos. "With the help of the doctor we arrived at the conclusion that the change was due to the expelling of the tapeworm. While in the majority of people this parasite causes a drop in body weight, in Maria it was having the opposite effect. Once she was free of it, the pounds began to melt away: in one year she went from 90 kilos to 60".

As a direct result of this weight loss Callas received hundreds of letters from women begging her to reveal her secret, while beauty clinics and food companies offered her astronomical sums of money for an exclusive patent on the 'Callas Formula', but she refused to divulge it.

Chicago 1955

In November 1955 Maria Callas made her American debut in Chicago, marking her return to the country where she was born. On 17 November she sang the last of three performances of *Madama Butterfly* at Chicago's Lyric Theater. A clause in her contract stipulated she was to be always physically protected from outsiders by a cordon of people around her. This was to prevent her becoming the victim of a possible lawsuit being brought against her by a certain Ed Bagarozy, an ex-lawyer turned impresario. It appeared that in 1947, when Callas was still in her mid-twenties, she had signed a contract with Bagarozy in New York granting him 10% of her gross earnings over the next ten years in return for any future engagements he might obtain. Now, eight years later, Bagarozy was claiming his pound of flesh: to be precise, $300 000 in unpaid commissions.

At the Lyric, as Callas was making her way to her dressing room, she was suddenly confronted by a process server holding a summons. To deliver the summons, he was required by law to make bodily contact, which he did by rudely pushing the summons into Callas' kimono, after which he left. Already drained emotionally by the opera's demanding finale Callas, now totally hysterical, hurled insults at his retreating form. The scene was captured by a waiting Associated Press photographer and within a short time the photo had appeared in every newspaper throughout the world: it showed a furious Callas, her face contorted with rage and her mouth wide open, screaming insults.

Callas next vented her anger at the Lyric's managers whom she accused of failing to protect her. Then through her lawyers she told Bagarozy that as he had failed to find her any engagements, she owed him nothing and refused to pay his claim. The case dragged on for four years but eventually a settlement was reached.

New York 1956

On the eve of her Met debut Callas was featured on the cover of *Time* magazine. In the accompanying article she was asked about the much-publicized rivalry between her and Renata Tebaldi. Callas replied:

"The day that my dear friend Renata Tebaldi sings Norma or Lucia or Anna Bolena one night and La Traviata, La Gioconda or Medea the next, only then will I consider her a rival. Otherwise it would be like comparing champagne with Coca-Cola".

Milan 1957

Harper's Bazaar had commissioned a photographer to take a series of photos of Callas wearing antique jewellery, the venue being Verdi's apartments in the Grand Hotel. A famous jeweller had loaned an emerald necklace and because of its great value had hired a detective to keep it under careful watch. Ruffled by the detective's constant presence, Callas asked the jeweller to send him away, but he refused, saying it was the detective's job to protect the necklace. "Then I'll buy it", exploded Callas, and making out a cheque for almost 20 million lire handed it to the astonished jeweller. "Now that it's mine', she told them, "you can both get out".

Edinburgh 1957

In 1957 the Scala company had been invited to perform *La sonnambula* at the Edinburgh Festival, with Callas as Amina. Four performances were scheduled, but because they were so successful La Scala asked her to sing a fifth. This fifth performance clashed with an invitation to attend a party in Venice given in her honour by her friend Elsa Maxwell, the gossip columnist. Having fulfilled the terms of her contract by performing the four scheduled performances Callas saw no reason why she should not attend the party and left Edinburgh the next day.

The Italian press, ready to pounce on Callas for the slightest misdemeanour, rose to the occasion. *"Callas breaks her contract with La Scala!"* screamed the headlines. The fact that she had not been contracted to sing this fifth performance was carefully omitted. As for La Scala, instead of issuing a statement confirming this, it chose to remain silent; matters were not helped by Elsa Maxwell publicly announcing that la Callas had 'cancelled' in order to attend her party. As a result Callas was again castigated as being unreliable and temperamental.

Rome 1958

Several months later there occurred the most damaging episode in Callas' entire career: the so-called 'walkout' at the Rome Opera. On 2 January she was to open the season with *Norma,* but two days earlier, while rehearsing in the unheated theatre, she caught a cold. To make matters worse, she had stayed up late at a New Year's Eve party and had inhaled a great deal of smoke. When morning came she found she had virtually no voice and could only speak in a whisper.

The night of the performance arrived. Being a Gala event, the theatre was sold out. In the audience were the President of Italy, Giovanni Gronchi and his wife. Despite feeling unwell Callas managed to get through the first act but was unable to continue. No understudy had been engaged and the performance came to a close. When this was announced pandemonium broke loose. Angry shouts of "You've cost us a million lire!" and "Go back to Milan!" came from the enraged audience, and Callas had to be escorted via an underground passage behind the stage to the adjoining Quirinale Hotel where she was staying. Her 'walkout' was reported as just another tantrum staged by the 'Tigress of the Opera' and consequently few theatres in Italy would now engage her.

An amusing sequel to the scandal, as reported in a Rome newspaper, was the story of a cheating husband who, on returning home late at night, gave his wife a glowing account of the entire performance - unaware that it had been cancelled after the first act!

Paris 1958

In view of Callas' diminishing reputation in Italy, her manager-husband Meneghini had arranged for her to sing in Paris. This was at a concert at the Opéra organised by the *Légion d'Honneur*. For this concert, the highlight of which was act 2 of *Tosca* with Tito Gobbi and the tenor Albert Lance, she received the highest fee ever paid to a singer: 5 million francs (this was before the introduction of the *new franc*). The 2130 seats, at 35 000 francs each, were sold within a few days; boxes fetched 300.000 francs; the program, which weighed one kilo, sold for 2000 francs; a dinner, served in the foyer for 450 VIP guests, cost 15 000 francs.

Attending were such luminaries as the president of France; ambassadors from Britain, Italy, the United States and Russia; the Duke and Duchess of Windsor; the Ali Khan; film stars Juliette Greco, Martine Carol, Brigitte Bardot and Charlie Chaplin; and even Aristotle Onassis. The entire concert was televised (later issued on DVD) and is regarded as the most prestigious musical event of the decade in France. At the end of the concert Callas returned her fee of five million francs to the *Légion d'Honneur* as her donation to a worthy cause.

Careers cut short

Several well-loved singers died tragically young, either as the result of illnesses or fatal accidents. Here's a short list taken at random *(see also Forza*: Warren*)*.

Wolfgang Anheisser, a promising German baritone, died onstage while on a swing, caused by a breaking rope. He was 44.

Giuseppe Borgatti, who created the role of *Andrea Chénier,* went on to become the leading Italian tenor of Wagnerian roles. During a rehearsal of *Tristan und Isolde* at La Scala he suddenly became blind and was forced to give up his stage career but continued to appear in concerts.

Sophie Braslau, popular American contralto, died from lung cancer at 43.

Lina Bruna-Rasa was coached by Mascagni for the role of Santuzza in the 50th anniversary recording of *Cavalleria Rusticana.* Following the death of her mother she developed schizophrenia and at the age of 30, while on stage, threw herself into the orchestra pit. She was confined to an institution for the rest of her life.

Armand Castelmary, French bass, collapsed and died during a performance of *Martha* at the old New York Met. He was 63.

Maria Cebotari created the part of Aminta in Strauss' *Die Schweigsame Frau* and sang in Vienna and Salzburg, being particularly admired in Mozart roles. She also made a successful movie career. A victim of cancer, she died at the age of 39.

Gervase Elwes came from an aristocratic English family. At one time he served in the diplomatic service. While touring North America in 1921 he fell under a moving train in Boston station and died; he was 32.

Kathleen Ferrier will always be lovingly remembered by both colleagues and public. Her career had only just taken off when she was stricken with cancer and died at the early age of 41. Fortunately her records bear testimony to her uniquely beautiful contralto voice, superb musicianship and sensitive interpretations.

In 1927 Romanian tenor **Trajan Grozavescu** stood at the threshold of a promising career, but after a performance at the Vienna Staatsoper his wife, in a fit of jealousy, took his revolver and shot him. At the court hearing she was acquitted as being of unbalanced mind, the result of a miscarriage. He was 33.

The news of the death of **Mario Lanza** literally made headlines all over the world. Dubbed 'The American Caruso', he had made an astonishing career not in opera, in which he had appeared only twice (Pinkerton in *Madama Butterfly*) but in films. His success was so phenomenal that after he made *The Great Caruso* he had become a millionaire at the age of 29. In 1957 he moved with his family to Rome, and it was here that he developed acute phlebitis in his right leg. He was admitted to a clinic for treatment but died there of a heart attack in October 1959. He was 38.

Maria Malibran was the daughter of Manuel Garcia, head of the celebrated Garcia family of singers. She died from severe injuries on 23 September 1836 after being thrown from her horse while out riding near Manchester; she was 28. At one time her name was romantically linked to that of Vincenzo Bellini who, by a curious coincidence, had died exactly one year earlier on 23 September 1835.

Grace Moore, the glamorous American soprano, enjoyed a successful career in both opera and films (*One Night of Love, Love me forever*). A member of the New York Met she had sung in Paris, London, Vienna, Amsterdam and Berlin. In 1947, as her plane was taking off from Copenhagen it crashed and she and the passengers on board were killed. She was 47.

Adolphe Nourrit, the great French tenor who created such roles as Arnold, Robert, Masaniello, Eléazar and Raoul, began experiencing vocal problems in 1837 resulting in depression. When a rival tenor, Gilbert Duprez, appeared on the scene Nourrit convinced himself that his career was finished. In 1839, in a fit of depression, he committed suicide by jumping off the roof of his lodging-house in Naples. He was 37.

Mado Robin (q.v.) the famous French coloratura soprano who is credited with singing the highest note ever recorded, died of leukemia in 1960 at the age of 42.

Meta Seinemeyer, the gifted German soprano who took an active part in the Verdi revival in Germany in the 1920s, was another victim of leukemia. On her deathbed she married the conductor Frieder Weissmann, who conducted most of her recordings, including those of Verdi and Puccini arias. She was 34.

Ludwig Schnorr, the German tenor who created the role of Tristan, suffered a fatal stroke six weeks later brought about by rheumatic fever. He was 29.

Conchita Supervia, glamorous Spanish mezzo of the 1920s and 1930s was, together with conductor Vittorio Gui, responsible for the Rossini revival in the 1920s. In 1931 she married an English industrialist and in 1936 entered a London nursing home to await the birth of her baby, but due to complications following childbirth both she and the baby died. She was 41.

One of the saddest cases of a career cut short was that of the brilliant young tenor **Fritz Wunderlich.** In 1966, while staying at a hunting-lodge in Heidelberg, he fell down the stairs, resulting in severe injuries which proved fatal. He was particularly loved in Mozart roles and in operetta, to which his romantic stage appearance and spontaneous singing style were well-suited. He was 36.

Enrico Caruso

Biographers often have the disconcerting habit of lifting facts from previous biographies without first checking their authenticity. In the case of Caruso, the world of opera had to wait until the year 1990 to discover the truth: that he was *not* the eighteenth of 21 children as had been claimed by every biography until then!

This claim was finally scotched by the author of a new biography, none other than Caruso's natural son, Enrico Caruso jnr (*Enrico Caruso: my father and my family;* Amadeus Press, Oregon 1990). In his carefully researched book, he points out that as Caruso's parents were married in

1866, it would be biologically impossible to produce 18 children within seven years (Caruso was born in 1873), a fact that had escaped all previous biographers. Caruso was actually the third of seven children, of whom five survived.

He made his debut at the age of 21 in a small theatre in Naples. When a photographer arrived the next day to take his picture Caruso was still in bed: his only shirt was at the laundry. Draping himself in a bedspread he posed proudly for his picture, which has since been reproduced in various biographies.

Caruso was a gifted caricaturist who could dash off cartoons on the backs of restaurant menus, theatre programs or anything else that was handy. Every week he drew one free of charge for the Italian weekly, *La Follia di New York.* When the editor of a rival publication offered him $50 000 a year to produce a caricature every week he turned it down. "Singing is my business", he told the astonished editor, "drawing is my hobby; but it's not for sale".

When the time came to renew Caruso's contract at the New York Met, a blank space was left for him to fill in his own amount. Although it was intimated that he could go as high as $4000 a performance, he modestly wrote only $2500; more than that, he said, would demand too much from him.

Caruso made two (silent) movies, *My Cousin* and *A Splendid Romance,* for each of which he was paid $100.000! In the first, he played the double role of a famous tenor and his impoverished cousin, a sculptor. The second film was never released, although stills from it have appeared in some Caruso biographies.

Claque

claque: a group of people hired to applaud, runs the dictionary definition. And therein lies the danger, because anyone with a big enough purse can 'buy' applause, irrespective of whether the performance is average, mediocre or downright appalling. Furthermore, the definition omits to mention that the claque can also be hired to disrupt a performance by emitting boos, hisses, whistling, catcalls and other sounds of disapproval.

Like hotel rooms or discreet *pieds-à-terre,* claques can be hired for the night, two nights or longer. In addition to singers, conductors and even theatre managements have been known on occasion to hire a claque. It begins with a meeting between the *chef de claque,* as he is called, and someone representing the singer or theatre management. Fees are agreed upon, advances made –monetary, not amatory -hands are shaken and the deal is on. Despite grumblings, claques continue to exist because singers, and especially conductors, much prefer the claque's well-regulated applause to the hysterical outbursts of undisciplined opera fans who applaud their idol in the middle of an aria, thereby disrupting the performance and creating bad feeling among the audience.

Claque members receive no fee for their services: their remuneration consists entirely of a free ticket. Occasionally claques make the headlines. In the late 1950s and early 1960s there were clashes between the rival claques of Maria Callas (q.v.) and Renata Tebaldi at La Scala, gleefully reported in the Italian press.

There have been cases when a well-directed claque has actually saved a performance from floundering due to an uninspired conductor or singers routinely singing their parts. And contrary to what the average opera-goer may think, there are claques in almost every major opera-house in the world, Milan's La Scala, New York's Met and Vienna's Staatsoper being no exception.

For an insider's view of life in the claque the reader is referred to Joseph Wechsberg's entertaining memoirs *Looking for a Bluebird,* an extract from which appears under *Gaffes and Goofs (q.v.).* For a diverting history of the claque see George Martin's *The Opera Companion.* One of the earliest claques, he writes, was employed by the Roman emperor Nero. When Nero sang at an amphitheatre in Naples, he was applauded by a claque consisting of five thousand men!

Although Caruso never employed a claque when he sang at the old Met, he was friendly with an old German named Schol, an umbrella-maker by day and the Met's *chef de claque* at night. Schol's loyalty to Caruso was such that when the tenor decided to appoint a guard outside the entrance to his apartment in the Vanderbilt Hotel to protect his privacy, Schol was rewarded with the task.

Q: Which opera qualifies for the title "A Claquer's Night Off?" **A:** *Parsifal. (Applause not allowed).*

Composers who sang

At least four composers were also accomplished singers.

Gioacchino Rossini (q.v.) liked to entertain his guests, not only with gourmet cuisine cooked by himself, but with singing his own compositions. These formed part of his famous *Samedi soirs*, held in his Paris apartment, and according to those present, his singing of 'Largo al factotum' was as good as any professional baritone. Attendance at these evenings was by invitation only, and the list of guests reads like a Who's Who in music: Auber, Liszt, Gounod, Bizet, Saint-Saëns, Rubinstein, Sarasate and Verdi among others. Another was the tenor Enrico Tamberlick, renowned for his *do dal petto*. Whenever Tamberlick arrived, Rossini instructed his major-duomo to make the tenor hang his top C on a coat hook downstairs before entering the salon and to collect it on his way out.

Jean-Baptiste Fauré, the eminent baritone who created the roles of Nelusko in *L'Africaine* and Hamlet in Thomas' opera, was a gifted composer of songs, among them 'Cruifix' and 'Les Rameaux', both of which were recorded by Caruso. He was also a frequent performer at Rossini's *samedi soirs*.

Reynaldo Hahn, composer of the operetta *Ciboulette* and of such popular songs as 'Si mes vers avaient des ailes', was also a competent light tenor. You can hear him on records accompanying himself in his own songs; in one called 'La barchetta' Hahn's breath control and agility are astonishing. He was also the author of *Le Chant,* a manual on singing.

Michael Balfe, Irish composer of *The Bohemian Girl* and 28 other operas, was also a successful baritone, appearing in Italy, France, Russia and England. His debut in Paris as Figaro in *The Barber* was applauded by Rossini himself.

Curiosities and Miscellanea

The score of Giordano's opera ***Andrea Chénier*** is written entirely in the key of C.

Fenella, the title-role in Auber's ***La muette de Portici,*** is performed not by a prima donna, but a prima ballerina. As the title indicates, Fenella is *muette,* or dumb.

Gaetano Donizetti (1797-1848) composer of over 70 operas, when told that Rossini had composed ***The Barber of Seville*** in 13 days, replied "Si, fu sempre pigrone!' ('yes, he always was a lazy fellow!')

When Meyerbeer was composing ***Le Prophète,*** roller skates were all the rage. With his flair for spectacular stage effects, Meyerbeer wrote a ballet scene in which the dancers performed to the music - on roller skates!

Lucrezia Bori, Spanish soprano, whose real name was Lucrecia Borja y Gonzalez de Riancho was, as her name suggests, a direct descendant of the Borgias.

Lauritz Melchior, the great Wagnerian tenor, liked to make sure people spelt his name correctly by presenting them with a card bearing this poem:

> *"There is a tenor big and jolly*
> *who's hardly ever melancholy*
> *There's just one thing can raise his ire*
> *to have his name spelt Melchoir*

> *Such carelessness will bring a roar*
> *of rage from Lauritz Melchior!"*

George Bernard Shaw, who as music critic for *The Star* wrote under the name of Corno di Bassetto, had been invited by a wealthy dowager duchess, better known for her loquaciousness than her musical knowledge, to share her box at Covent Garden for a performance of *Tristan und Isolde*. "I should be honoured", replied Shaw bowing gracefully, "I have never heard you in *Tristan*".

And talking of *Tristan,* a performance with Birgit Nilsson at the Met in 1960 boasted *three* tenors in the role, one for each act. The explanation? It was during the winter and all three tenors – Vinay, Liebl and da Costa - were sick and felt they couldn't sustain an entire performance. However, each felt he could survive one act, and so it was agreed. At the end all three tenors were applauded for 'saving the show'.

Selma Kurz, celebrated Viennese coloratura, was deeply superstitious. If she saw a chimney-sweep before a performance, she believed she would sing exceptionally well that night. Accordingly, her manager used to hire one to pass by her dressing-room before the opera began. One evening, seeing a chimney-sweep passing by, Kurz opened her purse and gave him a generous tip, whereupon the honest man said "Thank you, madame, but I've already been paid!".

Unusual in the history of opera is a work based on the life of an opera composer. **Alessandro Stradella** (1644-1682) who composed numerous oratorios, operas etc, led a somewhat adventurous life. At the age of 33 he abducted the fiancée of a Venetian nobleman. The couple fled to Turin, hotly pursued by a band of assassins, but they managed to escape and fled to Genoa. Here he became involved with a married woman whose wealthy brothers, prominent in local society, hired an assassin, and he was murdered in 1882 at the age of 38. *Alessandro Stradella*, an opera based on episodes in his life, was composed by Friedrich von Flotow, composer of the ever-popular *Martha*.

Stradella was once regarded as the composer of the concert aria *Pietà, Signore*, but it is now believed to have been composed by Louis Niedemeyer (1802-1861).

In 1952, when the great Wagnerian soprano Kirsten Flagstad, then 57, was recording **Tristan und Isolde**, she felt unsure about some of her high notes, especially her top C. Accordingly Walter Legge, EMI record producer, arranged for his wife Elisabeth Schwarzkopf to sing these few notes for her. They were so expertly spliced into the recording that it was impossible to detect them. In appreciation, Flagstad made her a present of a gold watch.

All would have been well had not some nasty-minded person blown the gaff. The matter was publicised out of all proportion and Flagstad, deeply resentful, vowed never to make another record. However, four years later she relented and faced the studio microphones again, this time those of Decca. The result was a sublime recording of the *Wesendonck Lieder*.

According to the memoirs of Dame Nellie Melba, the dessert known as **Pêche Melba** was created for her by the celebrated chef Auguste Escoffier. While she was staying at the Savoy Hotel in London, Escoffier sent her a little silver dish on which were peeled peaches on a bed of vanilla ice-cream, the whole covered in a sauce of raspberry purée. As she herself predicted, *Pêche Melba* would be long remembered after she had departed this world.

Mascagni's little-known opera **Le Maschere** has the curious distinction of receiving its premiere simultaneously in six Italian cities in 1901. Despite this much-heralded event – in Milan the cast included Carelli and Caruso and the conductor was Toscanini – it was not a success and in several cities it was actually hissed off the stage. Only in Rome, where it was conducted by Mascagni himself, did it achieve some kind of recognition, albeit short-lived. It uses *commedia dell'arte* characters.

Who was the world's highest-paid opera singer? Like *The World's Greatest Tenor* (q.v) there is more than one contestant to the title. Adelina Patti, darling of Victorian audiences, received $5000 a night (then about £1000) payable in advance: if it wasn't, *Madame* refused to sing. About 40 years later Caruso was to earn $15 000 a night (then about £3000) for appearing in concerts, while from records up to the time of his death in 1921 he earned over $2 million in royalties. See also Maria Callas (q.v.)

But the singer who claims to have been paid the world's highest fee, neither for appearing in concerts or in opera, was the English bass David Franklin. In his autobiography *Basso Cantante,* he relates he was the Commendatore in the 1939 Glyndebourne recording of **Don Giovanni.** In those days the opera was recorded on 78rpm records, for which he was paid the princely sum of £4 per side. Having sung on four sides, he earned £16, but when his cheque arrived it was for £20. He then recalled that when the Don invites the statue of the Commendatore to dinner, the latter accepts the invitation with the one word *Sì.* That one word, as Franklin gleefully remarks, made him for one glorious moment the highest-paid singer in opera history: who else was paid £4 for singing just *one* note?

Francesco Maria Piave, the librettist of **Rigoletto,** is credited with writing the words of 'La donna è mobile Strictly speaking, he didn't: they had been written 300 years earlier, in French, by none other than King François I, on whom the Duca di Mantova is modelled. The words, which sum up the king's cynical attitude towards women, may be seen today, etched into a window-pane in his château at Chambord in France. Piave's verses admirably reflect the cynicism of the original:

> *Souvent femme varie* La donna è mobile
> *bien fol est qui s'y fie!* qual piume al vento
> *Une femme souvent* muta d'accento
> *n'est qu'une plume au vent!* e di pensiero!

While on the subject of *Rigoletto,* how many opera buffs know that Maddalena has an aria in act 3 but which is not in the score? First sung at a performance in Brussels (in French) in 1857, the music was lifted from 'Il Poveretto', a song composed by Verdi ten years earlier. In the French version this became "Prends pitié de sa jeunesse' and in it Maddalena pleads with Sparafucile to save the Duke's life. It was rediscovered in 1977 and inserted into a performance in Belfast some months later, but apart from the present writer no one in Verdian circles was aware that it had started life as one of Verdi's salon pieces. For a full account the reader is referred to Julian Budden's *The Operas of Verdi*, volume 3, page.ix.

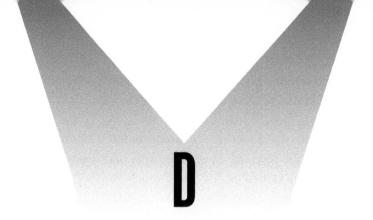

D

Debuts

Debuts can be dull affairs, leaving the audience indifferent, or they can be exciting events, with critics running out of superlatives.

Let's start with **Mary Garden**. While a student in Paris the Scottish-born soprano had attended rehearsals of *Louise* at the Opéra-Comique. After the premiere in 1900 she had attended so many performances (as a student she received free tickets) that she knew the words, music and stage movements by heart.

Two months later the creator of Louise, Marthe Rioton, became ill during a performance and Garden, who happened to be in the audience, was asked to take over the role. Despite objections from the conductor, who learnt that the unknown 26 year-old had never sung on stage before, she scored a great success. The next day she was offered a contract at 1000 francs a month. Garden went on to sing the role of *Louise* over 100 times and virtually made it her own.

Luisa Tetrazzini's London debut was delayed due to the machinations of Nellie Melba, who had used her considerable influence at Covent Garden to keep Tetrazzini out. But in 1907, when Melba was in Australia, Tetrazzini was engaged to sing Violetta. The press had not been notified and as the weather was cold and foggy the theatre was half-empty. But when Tetrazzini began 'Ah fors'e lui the audience knew that here was one of the greatest singers of the century. It is reported that the manager ran to the telephone to alert the newspapers to despatch critics immediately so that they could review the remainder of the opera.

Her performance was a success unprecedented in the annals of the Royal Opera House. She received 20 curtain calls and overnight became the undisputed prima donna of her time, much to Melba's chagrin. After reading about Tetrazzini's sensational debut, Adelina Patti, then 64, made the arduous journey from her castle in Wales to attend her next performance, after which she publicly proclaimed la Tetrazzini her successor.

Very different to these debuts was that of **Tito Schipa.** In 1909, barely 20 years old, the unknown tenor made his debut in *La traviata* at Vercelli. His fee? there wasn't one: he had to *pay* the impresario 20 lire for the privilege of singing Alfredo!

Perhaps the most sensational debut of all time was that of **Rosa Ponselle.** An unknown 21-year old from Connecticut, she was chosen by Caruso to sing opposite him in the Met's first production of *La forza del destino*. Although Ponselle had been singing in vaudeville with her sister Carmela, the opera stage was unknown to her. She was given five months to learn the role of Leonora, and received daily vocal coaching from Romano Romani, her mentor and friend. On 15 November 1918 she made her debut at the Met and despite first-night nerves scored a triumphant success, opening the doors to other American-born singers who previously were not accepted at the Met unless they had trained in Europe.

The youngest singer to make a professional debut was the Spanish mezzo **Conchita Supervia:** she was barely 15 when she sang in *Los amantes de Teruel* in Buenos Aires. The following year she sang, in Italian, Octavian in the Rome premiere of *Der Rosenkavalier*. This is probably the only instance in opera where the interpreter of Octavian is the same age (16) as the rose-bearer.

Tito Gobbi's Scala debut could hardly be called an auspicious occasion. As a 22-year old student at the Scala School for Young Singers, he was suddenly asked, a few hours before the performance, to sing the part of the Herald in the first performance of Pizzetti's *Orseolo*, the singer engaged having fallen ill. His 'part' was hardly challenging: it consisted of singing one line 'La Signoria del Doge e del Senato', to be delivered all on one note. Seems simple enough.

Unfortunately Gobbi knew nothing about the opera nor about the timing of his entrance. At the stage manager's signal he leapt forward onto the stage and ignoring the bass who was singing an aria shouted out his line as loudly as he could – at least *half a minute too soon!* The result was that the bass stopped dead, while Pizzetti, who was conducting, almost suffered a stroke! Returning to his dressing-room, Gobbi changed his costume, removed his make-up and made his ignominious way back to his pensione, shedding many tears *en route.*

Roberta Peters, the brilliant American coloratura soprano, made her debut at a few hours' notice. At the age of 20, and with no stage experience, she found herself virtually being pushed onto the stage of the Met to sing Zerlina in *Don Giovanni,* replacing an indisposed colleague. She was such a success that she became a member of the Met company, remaining with it for the next 30 years.

The following amusing anecdote was related to me in person by one of the participants so I can vouch for its authenticity.

Ljuba Welitsch made her Covent Garden debut as Salome in 1947. After acknowledging the applause from the cheering audience she made her way backstage to her dressing-room. As she was changing her costume there came a sudden knock on the door: a small group of male admirers had gathered outside to congratulate her on her spectacular performance. Taken totally by surprise, the somewhat flustered Bulgarian soprano, whose knowledge of English was rather limited at the time, called out:

Don't come in yet poys, I'm still dressed!

Joseph Schmidt's debut was somewhat unique. Being barely five foot tall (1.52m) a stage career was out of the question. Radio, however, had become the new medium and in 1929, aged 25, Schmidt auditioned for *Sender Berlin.* As he took his place behind the piano he almost disappeared from view: the piano was taller than he was, and when he announced he would sing 'Di quella pira' the studio staff burst out laughing: the thought of this little man singing one of opera's most heroic tenor arias was too much! But their laughter quickly turned to amazement as Schmidt's glorious tenor voice filled the studio and he was immediately offered a contract.

Definition

The definition of a true opera lover is someone who, on hearing the beauteous and shapely Anna Moffo singing in her bath, puts his *ear* to the keyhole...

And talking of *La Moffo,* she made her debut at 22 as Norina in Spoleto, and thanks to her brilliant lyric coloratura, stage presence, charm and stunning good looks she won immediate acclaim. Her next triumph was in *Madama Butterfly* on Italian television. This was such a success that it was followed up on TV by *Falstaff* and *La sonnambula.* This led to having her own TV program, *The Anna Moffo Show,* which made her even more popular in Italy.

In addition to her Violetta –a role she sang over 900 times – she was a noted Manon, Mimì, Lucia, Rosina and Gilda. She was also one of the few sopranos who could sing the four female roles in *Les Contes d'Hoffmann* and successfully bridge the gap between opera and operetta. In 1960 she was voted one of the ten most beautiful women in Italy.

Don Giovanni

The following was related to me personally by the late Ian Wallace, so I can vouch for its authenticity.

His finest role was Leporello, which he sang many times at Glyndebourne and elsewhere and, of course, nearly always in Italian. One year he received an invitation to sing the role in Parma. While singing 'Madamina' in act I the audience began laughing, and as this had never happened before he became somewhat alarmed, thinking perhaps that his costume was not done up properly – or worse! As he finished his aria to loud applause the reason suddenly dawned on him: for the first time he was singing to an audience *that understood every word!*

Encore

A term used when an audience requests that an aria be repeated; in Italy, France etc it's called a *bis*. Famous arias like 'La donna è mobile' or the sextet from *Lucia* were traditionally encored but in modern times the practice is eschewed, especially by conductors unwilling to compromise artistic integrity. When Toscanini was conducting *Un ballo in maschera* the Scala audience demanded that the popular tenor Giovanni Zenatello be allowed to repeat the quintet. Toscanini refused. When the audience started to boo he threw down his baton, stalked out of the opera house and went home. It took the Scala management three years to coax him back.

Falstaff

Attentive listeners may have noticed that when Falstaff sings his aria 'Quand'ero paggio del duca di Norfolk' he accents the second syllable of 'Norfolk' instead of the first. This mistake is generally attributed to Boïto who, it was assumed, wasn't aware of the misplaced accent. In fact, Boïto was an accomplished linguist and therefore well aware of it. In a letter to Verdi he explained that, in English, 'Norfolk' is stressed on the first syllable, as in 'Windsor' or 'Falstaff', but whenever he changed the stress the verse suffered. He therefore decided that the misplaced accent was the lesser of the two evils. Verdi accepted Boïto's explanation.

Kathleen Ferrier

This much-loved English singer, who in addition to possessing a most beautiful contralto voice was a highly competent pianist, was also extremely modest. Having a sparking sense of humour she liked to tell the following story.

Having been scheduled to sing at a concert in the Free Trade Hall in Manchester, and with time to spare, she decided to hop on a bus instead of taking a taxi. As the bus approached the Hall, crowds of people were milling about, trying to get in. As she was about to alight, the conductor said: "If you're thinking of going to the concert, luv, you'd better forget it. You'll never get in, the place is packed!"

On another occasion she had been engaged to sing at the Holland Festival in Amsterdam. As her aircraft approached the runway, she saw a reception committee waiting near the tarmac with a large bouquet of flowers. Turning to her companion she remarked: "There must be a VIP on board". It was only when the group approached that she realised the 'VIP' they were waiting for was *her!*

Footprints

Ever noticed how some popular songs of the past closely resemble well-known arias from operas? Here are a few examples:

The opening bars of *"I'll string along with you"*, made famous by Doris Day, is note-for-note identical to Radames' phrase in the love duet from act 3 of *Aïda*.

The refrain of *"Valentine"*, Maurice Chevalier's big hit, is virtually the same music as sung by di Luna's followers in act 2 of *Il trovatore* just before the count launches into *Per me ora fatale*.

The refrain of *"J'attendrai"*, the song made popular by Tino Rossi, is the same as the opening bars of the Humming Chorus from *Madama Butterfly*.

"Avalon", composed by Vincent Rose with words by Al Jolson, was the subject of a court case in 1921 involving a charge of plagiarism. Ricordi, Puccini's publisher, claimed that its opening bars were a copy of *E lucevan le stelle* from *Tosca*. For a full account see **Puccini**.

La forza del destino

Among singers, *La forza del destino* has the reputation of bringing bad luck. 'Forza', they say, possesses the *Malocchio,* or the Evil Eye, and invariably brings misfortune of one kind or another to those performing it, as Beniamino Gigli was to discover when he made his debut as Don Alvaro.

In act 1, Don Alvaro throws his pistol to the ground to show he is unarmed, but it accidentally goes off, killing Leonora's father, the Marquis. The noise of the explosion is provided by a stagehand firing an airgun, but when Gigli threw his pistol to the ground, nothing happened: the stagehand had fallen asleep! The Marquis, in an attempt to keep the stage action alive, fell to the floor mortally wounded, expiring shortly afterwards. While Gigli was bending over his body, lamenting his fate, a shot rang out thirty seconds later: the stagehand had woken up! The audience, of course, burst out laughing.

But worse was to come. In act 3 Don Alvaro, gravely wounded, is carried in on a stretcher. Unfortunately, one of the bearers lost his footing, the stretcher dropped to the ground and poor Gigli rolled ignominiously out of it. He had no choice but to pick himself up and climb back onto the stretcher, in full view of the audience, which by this time was helpless with laughter.

In act 4, disaster struck again. Don Carlos challenges Don Alvaro, who has now become a monk, to a duel. As Gigli bent down to pick up his sword, he heard a tearing sound: his skintight breeches had split up to the back! Fortunately, the damage was concealed from the audience by his monk's habit.

Forza's reputation as the harbinger of misfortune struck again on the night of 4 March 1960, but this time the result was a real-life tragedy. Leonard Warren, the great Verdi baritone, had just finished singing 'Urna fatale del mio destino' when he suffered a heart attack and collapsed onstage. The curtain was hastily lowered and a doctor was called but Warren was already dead. It then befell Sir Rudolf Bing, the Met's general manager, to inform a shocked audience that Warren had sung his last role; he was 49. In the cast that night were Renata Tebaldi and Richard Tucker, both close friends of Warren. As a sign of respect, the performance was halted and the audience, many of them in tears, made their way home.

G

Gaffes and Goofs

Of all the Performing Arts, none are surely more prone to mishaps than that of Opera, where the most tragic situation evolving onstage can be transformed within seconds into one of uproarious hilarity. As we have already seen, *La forza del destino* remains the hot favourite, closely followed by *La Bohème*. Here are a few more choice examples. First, from Peter Ustinov's introduction to Hugh Vickers' *Great Operatic Disasters,* reproduced by kind permission of the publishers:

In act 3 of *Götterdämmerung,* Siegfried's body is carried away on a litter by two pall-bearers. It so happened that shortly before the performance one of them was taken ill and was replaced by another who was new to the part. However, since all he had to do was to follow his mate onstage, lift the body onto the litter and carry it into the wings, it was decided for such simple stagework no rehearsal was needed.

The moment arrived. The two pall-bearers duly entered, lifted the body of the dead Siegfried and lowered it onto the bier. But when they picked it up, they found themselves facing each other. Lowering the bier, they each turned outwards, lifting it again, with the same result. It's not recorded whether the tenor singing the part of Siegfried was able to keep a straight face during these shenanigans but the Hamburg audience, roaring with laughter, gave the pair a warm round of applause.

Next is one which I witnessed myself. I was attending a performance of *Il trovatore* in the Italian provinces in which a friend was singing Leonora.

The chorus, consisting of six male and six female voices, had been recruited locally. As the curtain went up on act 2 it flashed through my mind what will happen when di Luna's men clash with Manrico's at the end of scene 2?

I need not have worried. As di Luna and his 'army of followers'– all six of them –lay in wait to abduct Leonora from the convent, Manrico appeared, but *sans* his followers. Reason? there being only six in the chorus, no more were available. Instead, at a sign from the conductor, di Luna's men split into two groups of three, one of which hurried over to join Manrico. A moment later the audience was treated to the hilarious spectacle of two groups of soldiers who, seconds earlier, had sworn allegiance to di Luna, drawing their swords and fighting each other to the death! Paid mercenaries couldn't have staged it better.

I have seen several unforgettable performances of *Il trovatore,* including one with Callas, one with Lauri-Volpi and one with Corelli, but for me the performance *in provincia* still remains the most unforgettable, albeit for different reasons.

In act 2 of *La traviata,* after the departure of Germont *père,* Violetta sits down at a table to write her acceptance of Flora's invitation. Then, following the stage directions, she reaches out to ring the bell for Annina. But a problem arises: the props manager had forgotten to provide it! Completely unfazed, Violetta boldly sang out *'Ting-a-ling!',* Annina duly appeared and the scene continued.

A few minutes later, but in another performance, the messenger who brings Alfredo Violetta's letter of goodbye from her carriage forgot to appear. Alfredo thought quickly, walked over to the table and finding some sheets of paper lying on it picked one of them up and sang *'Di Violetta!'.* The scene continued normally.

But gaffes don't happen only onstage. While singing Gilda at Covent Garden, Anna Moffo suddenly fainted after her opening duet in act 1 and the curtain was hastily lowered. Thinking it was the interval, some members of the audience seated in the stalls noisily left their seats and made their way to the bar, much to the derision of the remaining audience!

Rigoletto at Covent Garden again. As tenor Walter Midgley was launching into 'Questa o quella' the end of his moustache got caught up in his mouth and was slowly being sucked in. Somehow he managed to finish the aria and although the moustache was by now somewhere in his windpipe he succeeded in spitting it out, narrowly missing Borsa in the process.

For the next gaffe I am indebted to Joseph Wechsberg, author of *Looking for a Bluebird*, whom I once had the pleasure of meeting when he was correspondent for *Opera* magazine in Vienna. During his remarkably varied career he had been, *inter alia,* a ship's musician, a croupier and a member of the claque at the Staatsoper, which is where the following gaffe occurred.

Joseph Rogatchewsky, leading tenor of the Opéra-Comique in Paris, was making his debut at the Staatsoper as des Grieux in Massenet's *Manon*. It so happened that this role was the favourite of Alfred Piccaver, the darling of Viennese audiences. In act 3 Piccaver always sang a shortened version of 'Ah! Fuyez, douce image' and, as Wechsberg explained, it occurred to no one in the claque that Rogatchewsky might sing the complete version.

Act 3 came. After Rogatchewsky had sung the first part of his aria Schostal, the claque leader, gave the signal, with the result that [*quote*] 'a thunder of applause greeted the French tenor, who kept on singing, his beautiful *pianissimi* murdered by our brutal handclapping'. The next morning a repentant *chef de claque* made his way to Rogatchewsky's hotel but the tenor was a good sport. "Don't take it to heart" he told Schostal, "two times the applause is better than none at all".

The following was recounted by bass-baritone Ian Wallace. During the last act of *La Bohè*me, the singer who was playing Colline, who was dressed in an old-fashioned tailcoat with buttons on the back, leaned up against a table on which a small spirit lamp was burning. At the back of the lamp was a hook which somehow attached itself to Colline's rear just as he was making his exit. Spotting what had happened, Wallace closely followed him offstage to prevent the audience from seeing. When they got into the wings Wallace turned to him and said "What do you think you are? The 8.20 from Euston?".

Another incident involving a flame occurred during a dress rehearsal of *Tosca,* but unlike the one above, it was no laughing matter. In act 2, Maria Callas had her back against Scarpia's desk, her head hanging backwards. In doing so, her wig came in contact with the flame of a lighted candle. Alerted by the ensuing smoke Scarpia, played by Tito Gobbi, immediately went over and put his hand on the back of her head as if to draw her into an unwanted embrace, thus averting what would have been a highly dangerous situation. *"Grazie, Tito!"* Callas whispered.

A gaffe with a difference. During the last act of *Don Giovanni* in Dublin, the somewhat overweight Don got stuck in the trapdoor, leaving only his head and shoulders visible. *"Glory be!"* shouted a jubilant voice from the gallery, *'Hell's full!"*

While Columbia Records were recording operas at the Bayreuth Festival during the 1930s they ran out of 'waxes', blanks on which the recordings were made. An urgent cable was sent to London for a further supply but nothing arrived. On phoning the factory in an attempt to trace the missing waxes it was discovered they had been sent, not to Bayreuth in Germany but to *Beirut* in Lebanon!

Amelita Galli-Curci

Many singers owe much of their fame and fortune to the gramophone but Amelita Galli-Curci owed her international reputation entirely to records.

She made her American debut in Chicago, as Gilda, later adding Lakmé, Violetta, Juliette, Linda and Norina. From Chicago she went to the New York Met, where she created a sensation. Her voice, with its beautiful limpid quality, spontaneous delivery and ease of production, was perfectly suited to the recording techniques of the day and her records sold by the hundred thousand. She possessed, however, one serious defect, a tendency to sing flat, audible on several of her records, but as one critic remarked:

"Was there ever a soprano on record who sings so obviously out of tune and yet does it so endearingly?" In addition to solos from *The Barber of Seville, Rigoletto, Lakmé, Manon* and *Lucia* her duets with Giuseppe de Luca and Tito Schipa, recorded 90 years ago, continue to enchant the listener.

Giuditta, **opera in 3 acts, music by Franz Lehár",** states the Concise Oxford Dictionary of Opera. *"Giuditta, operetta in 3 acts, music by Franz Lehár"* says The Dictionary of the Opera. Which is correct? Up to a point, both.

Franz Lehár, composer of such world-famous operettas as *The Merry Widow, The Count of Luxembourg, The Land of Smiles* and many others, had always nursed ambitions to compose an opera. As early as 1896 he had written *Kukushka*, his first work for the stage, but it had little success. Now, 38 years later, and with a string of successful operettas behind him, he produced his crowning achievement. *Giuditta* was given its world premiere, *not* at the Metropol in Berlin, or the Theater an der Wien or the Volksoper, but the Staatsoper in Vienna.

This occurred on the evening of 20 January 1934 before a glittering first-night audience who had paid 'Caruso' prices – three times the normal ticket price – to hear Jarmila Novotnà and Richard Tauber (qv); the Vienna Philharmonic was conducted by the composer. Despite the hostile attitude of many critics, who felt *Giuditta* was unworthy of performance at Vienna's most prestigious opera house, it was an overwhelming success and was performed 42 times to sold-out houses.

But to get back to my question. In its structure *Giuditta* followed the usual Lehár formula: a pair of serious lovers, a pair of comic lovers, spoken dialogue and an exotic setting. The title-role was sung by a svelte, glamorous 25-year old soprano, Jarmila Novotnà, who looked, sang and acted the part perfectly. As for her seductive waltz song, 'Meine Lippen, sie küssen so heiss!' which she sings in an elegant nightclub, it brought the house down. In act 2, set in North Africa, as she stepped into a moonlit garden dressed in a shimmering white nightgown, an audible gasp came from the first-night audience: of delight from the men and shock from the women! How do I know? An elderly Viennese acquaintance who was present at that first performance remembered every detail.

As for the music *Giuditta* is distinctly operatic in style. Octavio's entrance song 'Freunde, das Leben ist Lebensvert!' daringly opens on a high A, while Giuditta's famous waltz song ends on a high B. There are also numerous other instances in the score that demand a high standard of operatic singing.

First produced during the politically turbulent 1930s, it was inevitable that *Giuditta* would be subject to political meddling. The first act, set in Italy, raised the ire of fascist dictator Benito Mussolini, who vociferously objected to Octavio, an Italian army officer, being portrayed as a deserter. To placate the enraged *Duce,* Lehár and his librettists were obliged to change the locale to an anonymous Southern fishing village near North Africa!

Antonio Gomes

Can you name offhand one opera by this composer? A contemporary of Verdi, Antonio Carlos Gomes was considered in his time a successful composer of operas, of which he wrote nine, most of them to Italian libretti and all showing unmistakable signs of the older composer's influence.

Gomes was Brazilian by birth, and thanks to a stipend granted him by the emperor Don Pedro II he was able to study composition at Milan's Conservatoire. He is best remembered today for *Il Guarany,* produced at La Scala in 1870, to be followed by *Salvatore Rosa, Maria Tudor* and *Lo schiavo;* the latter contains a tenor aria, 'Quando nascesti tu', made famous by Caruso, Gigli and Lauri-Volpi on records. He also composed operettas, songs and various pieces for piano. Gomes died in 1896 at the age of sixty.

Oscar Hammerstein I

The life of Oscar Hammerstein I, the penniless emigrant from Germany who built 13 opera houses, is the stuff from which legends are made. Arriving in New York in 1864 with barely two dollars in his pocket, the 16-year old got a job in a cigar-making establishment. Such was his genius that he soon invented a cigar-making machine. This invention made him a millionaire and with the proceeds he decided to build opera houses. His most famous, the Manhattan Opera House in New York, opened in 1906 and among its stars boasted such illustrious names as Nellie Melba, Mary Garden, Luisa Tetrazzini, Lina Cavalieri and John McCormack.

By 1910 the Manhattan Opera House had become such a rival to the New York Met that Hammerstein was offered over $1m to close it down, on condition that he produce no operas in America for the next 10 years. With the money from the Met he went to London and built the London Opera House (later The Stoll) but it was not a success and two years later it closed down. His grandson, Oscar Hammerstein II, is best remembered as the partner in the Rodgers and Hammerstein musicals.

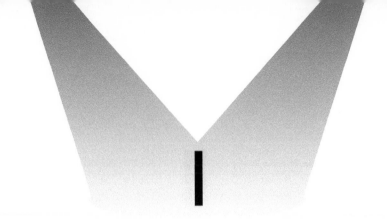

Interpolations and self-borrowings

Interpolations are pieces integrated into the score to provide local colour. Two famous examples are 'The last rose of summer', used by Flotow in *Martha*, and 'Home, sweet home', used by Donizetti in the Mad Scene of *Anna Bolena*,

Self-borrowings are more common. The overture to *The Barber* was lifted by Rossini from *Elisabetta, regina d'Inghilterra*, itself previously lifted from *Aureliano in Palmira*. Almaviva's serenade 'Ecco ridente' was also lifted from *Aureliano*, while the rondo finale to *La Cenerentola* was lifted from *The Barber* and re-titled 'Non più mesta'.

'Ach so fromm', Lionel's aria in Flotow's *Martha*, better know by its Italian title of M'appari', was lifted from an earlier opera L'âme *en peine*

'Gloire immortelle' the Soldiers' Chorus from Gounod's *Faust*, was lifted from a previous opera, *Ivan the Terrible*.

'Al dolce guidami', sung by Anna Bolena at the beginning of her mad scene, came from Donizetti's first opera *Enrico di Borgogna*

'Spirto gentil', Fernando's aria in *La favorita*, was taken from *Il Duca d'Alba*, left unfinished by Donizetti at the time of his death.

La Juive

Characters in opera are traditionally type-cast by voices: heroes are tenors, heroines are sopranos, fathers or villains baritones and basses. It therefore comes as a refreshing change to find that in one opera at least, the role of an old father is sung by a tenor. This is Halévy's *La Juive,* and the change came about through the request of a celebrated tenor of the time.

Adolphe Nourrit was a tenor who, in addition to possessing an heroic tenor voice, was blessed with musical intelligence. He had created the roles of Arnold in *Guillaume Tell,* Robert in *Robert le diable,* Masaniello in *La muette de Portici* and was the obvious choice for *La Juive,* after which he created Raoul in *Les Huguenots.* But Halévy had written the part of Eléazar, Rachel's father, for bass. Nourrit pleaded with Halévy to rewrite the part for tenor, arguing that he was tired of portraying romantic young heroes on stage, so Halévy agreed. Nourrit also wrote the words of Eléazar's great aria 'Rachel! quand du Seigneur.'

Gustave Kobbé

This eminent musicologist, critic and writer was the author of several books on opera, including a 2-volume work on Wagner. He is best remembered for his *Complete Opera Book*, first published in 1919; by 1950 it had notched up 20 printings and has influenced several generation of readers, more than any other English-language book on opera. In his capacity as music critic he attended the first performance of *Parsifal* at Bayreuth in 1892.

Due to a freak accident Kobbé never lived to see the publication of his *magnus opus*. In 1918, while sailing his boat near Long Island, a US Navy seaplane struck it as the pilot was trying to land and Kobbé was killed instantly.

Erich Wolfgang Korngold

Hailed as the *Wunderkind* of Austrian music at the beginning of the last century, Korngold achieved international recognition at the age of 12 with his *Piano Trio,* followed a year later by his ballet *Der Schneemann,* orchestrated by his teacher Zemlinsky. His opera *Die tote Stadt,* composed when he was only 23, starred the glamorous Maria Jeritza in the role of Marietta. In 1934 he emigrated to Hollywood, where over the next 12 years he composed 18 film scores.

Librettists

In the partnership between composer and librettist, the latter is very much the junior partner, and despite his invaluable contribution he often remains unrecognized. Who are these forgotten men? In earlier times, they were court poets, later writers, theatrical and literary people, authors in their own right. Mozart's favourite was Lorenzo da Ponte, whose official title was Court Poet to Emperor Joseph II of Austria. His three Italian masterpieces: *Le nozze di Figaro*, *Don Giovanni* and *Così fan tutte* bear testimony to his remarkable literary skills.

Felice Romani produced librettti for Rossini, Bellini and Donizetti. Verdi's principal librettists were Piave, Cammarano, Somma, Maffei and Boïto, who between them produced 16 libretti for the composer. Then there was the indefatigable – and aptly named – Scribe, who produced about 300 libretti for a whole range of composers, including Adam, Auber, Boieldieu, Donizetti, Gounod, Halévy, Meyerbeer, Rossini and Verdi. His capacity for churning out libretti on virtually any subject earned him the sobriquet 'The Scribe Factory'.

Puccini's principal librettists were Giacosa, Illica, Adami and Simoni, all well-known writers in their own right. Boïto, Leoncavallo and Wagner had no need of librettists: they wrote their own libretti. The theme of Richard Strauss' *Capriccio* is the age-old argument of whether the words are more important than the music.

Lucia di Lammermoor

Every opera lover knows that Donizetti's opera is based on Sir Walter Scott's novel *The Bride of Lammermoor*, and that Lucia, on her wedding-night, went mad either because she slew her husband or because she was accompanied by a flute – or both. What's not generally known is that Scott based his novel on an horrific tragedy that had taken place in Scotland in 1668, that is, some 150 years earlier.

Janet Dalrymple, daughter of the Viscount of Stair, had pledged herself to a Lord Rutherford. Her parents, however, opposed the match and she was forced to marry David Dunbar, Lord of Baldoon. On the wedding-night Janet was found crouching in the bridal chamber, her reason gone, while the unfortunate groom was found stretched out on the bed, covered in blood, having been stabbed several times. The bride never regained her sanity and died shortly afterwards, but the groom survived. Another version has it that Janet had been stabbed by either Dunbar or Rutherford, the latter seeking revenge for Lucia's so-called betrayal.

Madama Butterfly

This opera, based on a play, was in turn based on a novel. Having seen the play in London Puccini decided to use it for his next opera, and like *Lucia,* the novel was based on a true story, in this case one that had taken place in Japan. The real-life Butterfly, Tsuru Yamanura, was born in 1851. In Nagasaki she met a wealthy English businessman and bore him a son. When he left her she attempted *hara-kiri*, but survived; she died some years later at the age of 37.

Opera buffs who like to follow the libretto while listening to the recording may have noticed that, if their libretto *of Madama Butterfy* also contains a German translation, the hero's name is given as *Linkerton* instead of *Pinkerton*. No, it's not a misprint: *Linkerton* is also used in German-sung versions of the opera. It was changed because in German, *Pinkerton* has a mildly indelicate connotation. So to avoid bringing blushes to the cheeks of susceptible young *Mädchens, Linkerton* is used.

Maschere, Le

This little-known opera by Pietro Mascagni has the curious distinction of receiving its premiere simultaneously in six Italian cities in 1901. Despite this much-heralded event - in Milan the cast included Carelli and Caruso and the conductor was Toscanini – it was not a succes and in several cities it was actually hissed off the stage. Only in Rome, where it was conducted by Mascagni himself, did it achieve some kind of recognition, albeit short-lived. It uses *commedia dell'arte* names.

McCormack John

"An Irish tenor, singing Italian opera in New York? Sounds like a cinch!"

And how right Oscar Hammerstein (*q.v*) was when he engaged the 25-year old Irishman for his Manhattan Opera House. The 'cinch' was an immediate success and for the next 25 years McCormack was feted and idolised by millions of Americans, especially women, wherever he sang.

Ireland's greatest tenor was born in 1884, the fourth child of eleven children of whom only five survived. At the age of 19, totally unknown, he entered the tenor section of *Feis Ceoil*, a national singing competition held in Dublin. There were 14 competitors and McCormack was the 14th. The test-piece was Handel's 'Tell Fair Irene', and when he had finished, the adjudicator, the Italian composer Luigi Denza, who also taught singing at the Royal Academy of Music, rose and without hesitation awarded the young tenor first prize, a gold medal.

About two years later McCormack went to Italy to study with the celebrated teacher Vincenzo Sabatini, making his official debut three months later in the title-role of Mascagni's *L'Amico Fritz*. In the last act he has the aria 'O amore, o bella luce del cor', the climax of which is a high B flat. Scared of singing it McCormack, to quote his own words, "I opened my mouth wide, struck a dramatic pose and pretended to sing the note", but didn't produce any sound". The ploy worked; the audience, thinking he had sung a fortissimo B flat, applauded loudly and demanded a *bis!*.

After two years of study McCormack, now married to Lily Foley, returned to England. At Covent Garden he was offered the role of Turiddu, becoming the youngest soloist – at 23 – to sing there. Two weeks later he scored an even greater success as Don Ottavio. His singing of 'Il mio tesoro' was highly praised by critics, while his famous recording of the aria bears testimony to his exemplary diction, phenomenal breath control and excellent phrasing.

Despite his success in opera, McCormack was never comfortable on the operatic stage. Critics carped about his poor acting – he himself admitted he was a bad actor - and in 1912 he decided to give up the stage and concentrate almost exclusively on the more lucrative business of concerts. It was a wise decision, artistically and financially. At the New York Hippodrome, for example, he sang to audiences of 7000 and at the Met to over 5000. These were always sell-out performances and hundreds of disappointed fans were turned away. His silver tenor voice was also ideally suited to recording and his Victor Red Seal records sold by the hundred thousand.

Having made his career in America McCormack became a U.S. citizen. By 1921, following the death of Caruso, he was acclaimed America's most popular classical singer. It has been estimated that at the height of his popularity he was earning something like one million dollars a year: not bad for someone who, barely thirty years earlier in his native Ireland, received three guineas for his first engagement.

McCormack's wealth allowed him to indulge in his love of art and painting. Among others he owned a Corot, a Frans Hals, a Rembrandt, a Greuze and a Gainsborough. A devout Catholic all his life, he was created a Papal Count in 1928 in recognition of his generous contribution to Catholic charities.

Like his famous contemporary Richard Tauber *(q.v)* McCormack was constantly under attack from critics who deplored his singing of inferior types of music, particularly sentimental Irish songs and ballads. "I suppose you think I sing nothing but muck!" he once told Sir Compton MacKenzie, editor of *The Gramophone*. The point is that like Tauber he brought to these lesser items the same degree of musicianship and artistry that he gave to songs by Mozart, Schubert or Wolf.

His concert tours took him to almost every part of the world, including Europe, Australia, Asia, China, Japan and South Africa. While touring

Japan McCormack happened to pass a record shop playing his recording of 'O sleep, why dost thou leave me' at a very fast speed. "You're playing that much too fast," McCormack told the dealer. "Oh, no sir", he replied, "ees good; ees great singer John Comic".

McCormack retired in 1938 and died seven years later aged 61. He was happily married to Lily for about 40 years and they had two children, Cyril and Gwen. When Cyril was asked if he wanted to be a singer like his celebrated father he replied "Oh no; I'm going to *work!*".

Name-changes

Many famous opera stars who, like their Hollywood counterparts, were born with ordinary-sounding or unpronounceable names, changed them to further their careers. Joe Bloggs won't get you far in opera, but changing it to Giuseppe Bloggini might. Here's a list of name-changes, by no means complete.

Maria Callas	Maria Kalogeropoulos
Mario Chamlee	Archer Cholmondeley
Eleonora de Cisneros	Eleanor Broadfoot
Jean de Reszke	Jan Mieczislaw
Emmy Destinn	Ema Kittlová
Louise Edvina	Marie-Louise Martin
Elise Elizza	Elisabeth Letzergroschen
Benvenuto Finelli	Bennett Finn
Alma Gluck	Reba Fiersohn
Kathryn Grayson	Zelma Hedrick
Maria Ivogün	Ilse von Günther
Maria Jeritza	Maria Jedlitzka
Eduardo di Giovanni	Edward Johnson
Mario Lanza	Alfredo Cocozza
Aroldo Lindi	Arnold Lindfors
George London	George Burnstein

Riccardo Martin	Hugh Whitfield
Nellie Melba	Helen Mitchell
Lauritz Melchior	Lebrecht Hommel
Zinka Milanov	Zinka Kunc
Lillian Nordica	Lillian Norton
Jan Peerce	Jacob Perelmuth
Rosa Ponselle	Rosa Ponzillo
Rosa Raisa	Raitza Burchstein
Emma Renzi	Emmarentia Scheepers
Titta Ruffo	Ruffo Titta
Richard Tucker	Reuben Ticker
Beverly Sills	Belle Silverman

Others kept their names but changed them to suit the circumstances. When Jussi Björling used to sing with a dance band in his early days he became Erik Oddes; John McCormack sang in Italy as Giovanni Foli; Marie Powers, in Europe, became Maria Crescentini; Dora Labbette, English soprano, became Lisa Perli at a Covent Garden production of *La Bohème:* and Oda Slobodskaya, when appearing in operetta, became Odali Careno.

Nipper

Who's Nipper, you may ask, and what's he got to do with opera? It would be no exaggeration to say that Nipper is probably the most famous dog in the world, his picture having appeared literally everywhere. Although his story has been told before, some readers may not know it.

Nipper was the name of a fox terrier belonging to an English painter, Francis Barraud. In 1899, Barraud visited the offices of the Gramophone Company in London to borrow a brass horn, of the type fitted to the company's latest gramophone. The reason for his request was as follows.

Some years earlier, when Nipper was still alive, Barraud had painted an endearing picture of the dog as he sat listening to an Edison phonograph. It should be explained that Edison phonographs, which played cylinder records, were able to record voices as well as play them back. When Barraud played a cylinder record of his brother's voice - his brother was the previous owner of the dog - Nipper came and sat in front of the horn. Struck by the extraordinary appeal of the scene Barraud painted it, calling it 'His Master's Voice', but despite its originality there were no buyers and the painting was forgotten.

The years passed. One day a friend of Barraud, catching sight of the painting, now covered in dust, in his studio, suggested that it be updated by replacing the ugly black horn of the Edison with one of the shiny brass horns then in vogue – hence Barraud's visit to the Gramophone Company. The horn duly obtained, Barraud painted out the black horn, painted in the gleaming brass horn and returned a few days later to show the result to the manager, William Owen. Much taken by the painting, Owen offered to buy it, on condition that the rival Edison phonograph be replaced by the company's latest model gramophone. Barraud, happy to oblige, returned two days later with the painting, which now depicted the new gramophone and horn in place of the old phonograph, and was paid £100. Within a short time "His Master's Voice' had become the most famous trademark in the world. As for Francis Barraud, he earned a comfortable living for the rest of his life painting commissioned replicas of a little fox terrier, head cocked to one side, sitting in front of a horn, listening to the sound of his master's voice - proof once again that a dog is Man's best friend.

Le Nozze di Figaro

Did you know that Mozart's opera is based on an 18th century play that was considered so dangerous that it was initially banned? And that when it was performed four years later it contributed in no small way to promoting the liberal ideas that culminated in the French Revolution?

Le Mariage de Figaro was written by Pierre Augustin Caron, better known as Beaumarchais, a character as colourful and resourceful as Figaro himself. A watchmaker by profession, Caron began his career by teaching the harp to the four daughters of King Louis XV. He then became, in turn, secret agent to the same monarch, playwright, banker, publisher, gun-runner, librettist and amateur composer. By marrying the widow of an elderly courtier, from whom he had previously purchased a court title, he was able to enter the *beau monde*, and thanks to his friendship with a prominent Paris banker became extremely wealthy.

Le Mariage de Figaro was not intended to be a revolutionary play. Beaumarchais wrote it to show how a quick-witted barber of humble origin gifted with intelligence was the superior of an aristocrat whose sole purpose in life was pursuing women. In particular, Beaumarchais set out to ridicule the ancient custom of the so-called *Droit du Seigneur*. After the four-year ban was lifted the play had an enormous success, running to 68 performances.

Jacques Offenbach

This prolific composer, author of over 100 operettas and other stage works, was born in Cologne, Germany. Music poured out of him in such abundance that he frequently composed while holding a cup of coffee in one hand and feverishly writing down the music with the other. He even fitted out his carriage with a writing-desk so that he could write down music as it came to him while travelling. Having a bizarre sense of humour Offenbach liked to sign his name *'O de Cologne'*.

Opera in translation

The pros and cons of opera in translation are far too complicated to warrant inclusion here, but the following example shows the dangers that may be lurking…

A new English translation of *Madama Butterfly* was being used at the Met for the first time. In act 1, Sharpless asks Butterfly "Have you any sisters? - a correct translation of "E ci avete sorelle?" It was observed, however, that this seemingly innocent question provoked loud sniggers from the male sections of the audience: the sight of a middle-aged American consul asking a beautiful young ex-geisha if she had any sisters was sure to be misunderstood! Accordingly, at the next performance the question was changed to 'Have you any brothers or sisters?'.

Operas never written

The list of operas embarked upon but later abandoned is a long one. Verdi, for example, toyed for years with writing an opera on Shakespeare's *King Lear*, and even made sketches of the music, but in his methodical way all were destroyed. It is believed, however, that the words of a surviving sketch of a cavatina for Cordelia are almost identical to those sung by Leonora in act 1 of *La forza del destino*.

Puccini's list is the longest. Ouida's *Two Little Wooden Shoes* was one of the first casualties. His publisher Ricordi bought the rights but Puccini soon lost interest and Ouida's novel became Mascagni's *Lodoletta*. Next was *La Lupa* (The she-wolf) by Giovanni Verga, whose *Cavalleria Rusticana* had been previously used by Mascagni. Puccini actually went to stay with Verga in Sicily for several weeks to discuss the libretto and absorb the local atmosphere, but on his return to Torre del Lago his enthusiasm began to wane and *La Lupa* was abandoned.

La femme et le pantin, by Pierre Louy, was another victim. The heroine, Conchita, is a Carmen-like figure but intensely sadistic. Although Puccini commissioned Luigi Illica to prepare a libretto he gradually became more disenchanted and soon Conchita joined the heap of other discarded heroines. Riccardo Zandonai then used it for his verismo opera *Conchita*.

Orfeo ed Euridice

Characters in opera are traditionally type-cast according to voice; the exception is Gluck's *Orfeo ed Euridice*. Orfeo has been sung by no fewer than five different voices: soprano, tenor, mezzo, contralto and baritone.

I Pagliacci

When Canio and his troupe of players enter the village of Montalto he invites the villagers to attend the performance that night with the words *Un grande spettacolo a ventitre ore.* Despite the absurdity of a village performance starting at twenty-three hours, many writers, including translators of librettos, mistranslate this as 11 o'clock; the correct time in fact is 7 o'clock. The explanation is as follows.

In parts of southern Italy such as Calabria, where the action of the opera takes place, time was measured not by a clock but by the rays of the sun. Since sunset typically occurred at around 8pm, indicating the end of a 24-hour day, it came to be regarded as 24 hours; accordingly, 23 hours corresponds to 7 o'clock. Gustave Kobbé, (q.v.) in the early editions of his *Complete Opera Book*, got it right when he wrote 7 o'clock, but in subsequent editions edited by the late Earl of Harewood, it was 'corrected' to 11 o'clock, thereby misinforming an entire generation of readers. Other writers on opera, unaware of this local custom, continue to perpetuate this error.

Another example of this Southern way of telling the time is provided by the opening lines of the Neapolitan song *Senza nisciuno* by Ernesto de Curtis, which begin:

Tramonta 'sole, vintiquattore	**The sun is setting, twenty four hours**
e suona Ave Maria	**and the Angelus rings**

Canio's closing line 'La commedia è finita', has also been the subject of controversy. In earlier productions it was always spoken by Tonio who, it will be remembered, opens the opera with the prologue. It was Caruso who, realising its dramatic impact, begged the composer to give it to Canio instead, with whom it remained for about 50 years until Franco Zeffirelli restored it to Tonio at a Covent Garden production in 1959.

At a performance of *I Pagliacci* in the Italian provinces, the baritone singing the role of Tonio sang the prologue so badly that he was booed mercilessly by the irate audience. Poking his head through the curtains he said: "If you think I'm bad, wait till you hear the tenor!"

Jan Peerce

In 1953, while singing at the Cincinnati Zoo Summer Opera Festival, famed tenor Jan Peerce noticed a chubby 10-year old kid hanging around rehearsals. At the end of the season the boy produced an autograph book and asked Peerce to sign it, which he did without much enthusiasm.

About 15 years later Peerce was in Michigan, to take part in a concert version of *Rigoletto*. As he entered the hall where the rehearsal was taking place he heard someone playing the *Rigoletto* score beautifully on the piano. When Peerce asked Cornell Macneil, who was singing the title-role, the pianist's name, Macneil replied: "Don't you know him, Jan? he says he knows you very well". Peerce was sure he didn't know who the stocky, bushy-haired pianist was until he jumped up from the piano stool and running over embraced Peerce with the words "Jan! what a great day this is! It's a moment I've always dreamed of!" As Peerce still failed to recognize him the pianist produced an autograph book and opening one of the pages showed him the inscription which read:

> *"To James Levine, a worthy colleague, wishing you*
> *great success in your future. Jan Peerce, July 1953".*

Politics in Music

Politics in music can work both ways. When Auber's *La muette de Portici* was given in Brussels in 1830, the audience was roused to such a pitch of patriotic fervour that it sparked off the revolution which eventually led to Belgium's independence from the Netherlands.

On the other hand, the sheer lunacy of politics in music is shown by the following. One of Beniamino's Gigli's favourite arias was 'O Paradiso' from Meyerbeer's *L'africana,* which he often sang to open his recitals. Then politics stepped in. Following Mussolini's pact with Hitler in 1938, racial laws were introduced into fascist Italy. Because Meyerbeer was Jewish, "O Paradiso' was banned from public performance and recordings of it were deleted from Italian record catalogues.

Perhaps the most notorious case of racial discrimination was the one involving the famous black American contralto Marian Anderson, more so as it occurred in her own country. Despite her international reputation – she had sung in London, Paris, Vienna, Salzburg and Moscow - she was refused permission to give a concert at Constitution Hall in Washington D.C. by an organisation calling itself the Daughters of the American Revolution (DAR), who based their opposition on racial grounds. Their announcement provoked fierce condemnation and Eleanor Roosevelt, wife of the American president, sent her resignation to the DAR. Anderson was publicly supported by such eminent fellow artists as Kirsten Flagstad, Lawrence Tibbett and Jascha Heifetz, as well as various musical organisations throughout America.

The impasse was solved by her manager Sol Hurok, who organised an open-air concert on Easter Sunday 1939 at the Lincoln Memorial. Over 75 000 people attended and the concert was broadcast live. Sixteen years later Marian Anderson became the first black singer to appear at the Met, singing the role of Ulrica in *Un ballo in maschera.* During her career she received numerous awards, including honorary degrees from Princeton and New York Universities and the American Freedom Medal. For her 75th birthday a gold medal was struck in her honour.

Rosa Ponselle

"How does one get a voice like Ponselle's?" Lotte Lehmann is said to have once asked Geraldine Farrar. "By special arrangement with God," came the reply.

Considered the greatest dramatic coloratura soprano of her time – perhaps of all time - Ponselle's was a dark, rich and exciting voice, seamless throughout its entire range. Her nobility of style made her the ideal interpreter of operas by Spontini, Bellini and Verdi. She was born in the United States from an immigrant Italian family and such were her musical gifts that at the age of 10 she was already proficient on the piano. At 14 she was playing the piano in theatres showing silent movies, after which she teamed up with her sister Carmela as a singing duo act in vaudeville. It was here that she was seen and heard by none other than Caruso, who, despite her lack of opera experience, offered her the leading role of Leonora in *La forza del destino*, to be produced at the New York Met later that year. Having had no formal vocal training she studied every day with a coach for five months and in 1918 made a successful debut opposite Caruso at the Met. She was 21.

In 1936 she set her sights on Hollywood, where for her MGM film test she sang two arias from *Carmen*. When asked about her fee she coolly replied "a quarter of a million dollars!" After the studio manager had picked himself up from the floor there was a long silence. When she had left he said to his assistants "Is she crazy or am I? not even Clark Gable gets $250 000!". That was the end of Ponselle's Hollywood career; a year later she quit The Met and retired to her home *Villa Pace* in Baltimore. Her MGM film test was reissued on a DVD called *The Art of Singing*.

Prima Donnas

There are probably more anecdotes about prima donnas than any other personage in opera. Here's a selection that makes fascinating reading.

We begin with **Adelina Patti** who, in many ways, personified what a prima donna should be. In a career lasting 50 years Patti's title was the Queen of Song, and indeed, she looked like a queen, dressed like a queen – often wearing a tiara, and behaved like one. On tour, she travelled by train in her own private carriage which was fitted out with sleeping quarters, a kitchen and a grand piano. Her fee was $5000 a concert, and if it was not paid in advance she refused to sing. When she retired, she became baroness Cederström and lived in her castle in Wales.

Patti's successor was **Nellie Melba.** For 35 years she was the reigning queen of Covent Garden, powerful enough to keep out rival sopranos for many years. Although blessed with an exceptionally beautiful voice she was a poor actress. It was said of Melba that to depict happiness she would raise her left arm and to depict anger she would raise her right arm.

Melba liked to refer to herself in the third person. When asked to sing at a morning concert she hautily replied "Madame Melba does not sing at morning concerts". On another occasion she and John McCormack had been singing together at Covent Garden. When the final curtain came down he stepped forward to receive his share of the applause, only to find himself being rudely pushed back. "No one at Covent Garden takes a curtain call with Melba!" she told him angrily.

Melba's rival was the brilliant coloratura **Luisa Tetrazzini** (qv). Melba had succeeded in keeping her out of Covent Garden for years but in 1907, when Melba was in Australia, Tetrazzini was engaged for the Autumn Season. She created such an overnight sensation as Violetta that she became the toast of the season. Melba was furious but could do nothing, Tetrazzini now being firmly entrenched.

Both prima donnas used to stay at the Savoy Hotel during the opera season. On one occasion, Melba had arrived before Tetrazzini and could be heard warming up her voice in her apartment. As Tetrazzini was being escorted to her apartment by the manager she passed by Melba's rooms. Turning to the manager she asked sweetly "Sir, do you keep many stray cats in your hotel?"

"The World's Most Beautiful Woman" was how Italian soprano **Lina Cavalieri** liked to describe herself. Renowned more for her beauty than for her voice, she began life selling flowers in the streets of Rome and singing in sidewalk cafés. When she was barely 16 her beauty caught the eye of a wealthy Russian prince who married her. Thanks to his wealth she was able to study singing in Paris and within a few years was singing opera in Naples, Paris and St Petersburg.

In London, she auditioned for Henry Higgins, manager of Covent Garden. "And what fee had you in mind?" he asked, to which his beauteous visitor replied "£300 per performance" – unheard of at that time. With typical English understatement Higgins turned to the interpreter and said: "Would you kindly explain to the young lady that here at Covent Garden we are only engaging her to *sing*".

Cavalieri was married four times, one of her husbands being the French tenor Lucien Muratore. Her death in 1944 could have come from a modern opera. In WW2, during an air raid on Florence, she was on her way to a bomb-shelter when she decided to return to her villa to collect her jewels. A bomb fell on the villa and she died instantly. An Italian film on her life, *La donna piu' bella del mondo,* starring Gina Lollobrigida, was made in 1957 and has been reissued on DVD.

Mary Garden, while attending a dinner party given in her honour, was wearing a beautiful new gown with a daringly revealing *décolleté*. Sitting opposite was a man who couldn't take his eyes off her dress. "Tell me, Miss Garden" he asked, "what keeps your gown up?" Came the prompt reply "Your age and my discretion!".

The name **Florence Foster Jenkins** may not be familiar to opera lovers for the simple reason that she never sang in opera. She gave concerts instead, and being an extremely wealthy woman could afford to hire such prestigious venues as the Ritz-Carlton Hotel. At first her audiences consisted of a few loyal women friends but as word spread it became impossible to get tickets; they sold out within hours.

Was she that good, you may ask? The only person who thought so was Madame Foster Jenkins herself; the rest of the musical world thought she was hilarious. Audiences attending her concerts did so to have a good laugh, while critics in their reviews vied with each other in writing ambiguous comments such as:

"Never before have we heard a voice like that of Madame Foster Jenkins"

"I predict that this century will never produce another voice to compare with that of Madame Foster Jenkins"

"Inimitable'. "Hearing is believing", and so on.

Finally, at the age of 76, she hired Carnegie Hall. It too was sold out within a few days – no mean achievement, taking into consideration the seating capacity of about 2500. She died a month later, but her recorded voice can still be heard on a CD, *The Glory (???) of the Human Voice.* Her recording of the Queen of the Night's aria from *The Magic Flute,* sung in Italian, must be heard to be believed...

The prima donna *par excellence* as far as personal beauty, stage presence and temperament are concerned was undoubtedly the glamorous Moravian soprano **Maria Jeritza**. A beautiful, tall, blue-eyed blonde, she was also a consummate singing-actress who appeared during the 1920s and 1930s in leading roles and in newspaper headlines with equal frequency.

As Puccini's favourite Tosca, she first attracted attention at the Vienna Staatsoper in 1913. During rehearsals supervised by the composer himself, she accidentally slipped while struggling to free herself from the evil Scarpia's grasp and found herself lying face downwards on the floor. Instead of getting up, she sang Vissi d'arte in a prone position, gaining Puccini's whole-hearted approval and setting a precedent for future generations of Toscas.

About 12 years later came her much-publicized spat at the New York Met with Beniamino Gigli. The two had been cast in Giordano's *Fedora,* a role Jeritza had made very much her own. Towards the end of the opera

Count Loris, played by Gigli, has to push Fedora violently away from him. Whether Gigli miscalculated his force or whether she slipped remains unknown, but the frightened soprano found herself reeling towards the edge of the stage, barely saving herself from tumbling into the orchestra pit, straining her wrist and sustaining abrasions on both her legs. 'He did it!' she shrieked at poor Gigli, 'He wanted to kill me! Murderer! Murderer!' Gigli maintained it was simply an accident and the matter was settled when the Met issued a statement supporting him.

A fortnight later came the *Tosca* incident. On this occasion, an argument ensued about sharing applause after the final curtain. Stepping in front of the curtain, Jeritza announced to the audience *"Gigli not nice to me!"*; then collapsed sobbing into the arms of the conductor. Met manager Gatti-Casazza was called and spent the next two hours trying to pacify the hysterical prima donna. The next morning he announced that Jeritza and Gigli would never sing together again at the Met.

A year later, when Jeritza sang the part of princess Fedora at Covent Garden, she insisted on wearing her own jewels valued, in today's terms, at over a million pounds. To ensure their safety detectives from her insurance company, dressed as men of title, mingled onstage while keeping a watchful eye on her sparklers.

Maria Jeritza was married four times. She lived to be 95 and at every opening night at the Met she could be found seated in the front row of the stalls, immaculately gowned and graciously acknowledging the attention that was bestowed upon her.

According to *The Guinness Book of Records*, the highest note ever sung was by the brilliant French coloratura soprano **Mado Robin** who, believe it or not, could sing C above top C! After her debut as Gilda at the Paris Opéra in 1945 she added Lucia, Lakmé and Rosina to her repertoire. While singing in *Rigoletto* in San Francisco she decided to interpolate a high E in the duet that closes the second act. The conductor, caught unawares, threw down his baton in disgust and stalked out of the theatre; it took the management an hour to persuade him to return and continue the performance. You can hear Mado Robin sing a B flat above top C in her recording of the Mad Scene from *Lucia di Lammermoor.*

And talking of *Lucia,* when **Joan Sutherland** was rehearsing the part in the Met's ancient production, she couldn't help noticing the number of candelabras ablaze in the Wedding Scene. Turning to a friend she said "Liberace would be livid!"

When **Lilian Nordica** was singing at Bayreuth, she asked a friend to contact the great Lilli Lehmann, also appearing at the Festival, so that Nordica could make a social call. "I'm not taking any new pupils this season", the diva snapped back.

A pupil who *was* accepted by Lilli Lehmann was the native-born American beauty **Geraldine Farrar.** At the age of 19 she made her debut in Berlin as Marguerite in *Faust,* followed by appearances in Paris, Monte-Carlo and London, and returned in triumph to New York in 1906, where she became the Met's reigning prima donna, partnering Caruso in 16 seasons. She also created the title-roles in Giordano's *Madame Sans-Gêne* and Puccini's *Suor Angelica.* After Caruso's death in 1921 and with the advent of such rivals as Ponselle, Muzio and Jeritza at the Met, she retired the next year at the early age of 40. Her farewell performance as Zazà was attended by hundreds of 'Gerryflappers' – teenage girls screaming for their matinée idol. She was carried triumphantly aloft along Broadway draped in a lavish evening gown and wearing a crown and sceptre.

In her time she was a celebrated Butterfly, Tosca and Carmen. To the latter she brought to her stage performances several gimmicks she had picked up while filming *Carmen* in Hollywood, such as slapping Caruso's face in act 2, much to the tenor's dislike. A curiosity among record collectors is Farrar's recording of the love duet from *Madama Butterfly* with Caruso as Pinkerton. The story goes that Caruso arrived at the Victor studios in a mild state of inebriation. When he sang his line "Io t'ho ghermita, ti serro palpitante, sei mia!" Farrar, instead of replying "Sì, per la vita!" is reputed to have sung "He's had a highball!" The story did the rounds for years but in her autobiography *Such Sweet Compulsion* she denies it. It has been claimed that she did indeed utter these words but that the Victor company used a second 'take' which contained Farrar's "Sì, per la vita!" duly restored.

Giacomo *Puccini*

In 1907, Puccini was invited by the New York Met to supervise productions of *Manon Lescaut* and *Madama Butterfly,* both of which were being presented for the first time. One fine day, to use an operatic idiom, Puccini was strolling along Fifth Avenue when he saw displayed in a large showroom a motorboat that was his dream. Unfortunately, the price was also a dream: $3000. Puccini longed to buy the boat but gave up the idea as being beyond his means Fate, however, had other plans. The same evening he had been invited to a party. Also present was a millionaire who told Puccini that he was a great admirer of his operas and that he would be prepared to pay handsomely for an autographed copy of Musetta's Waltz Song from *La bohème.* "Three thousand dollars?" asked Puccini. "Done!" was the enthusiastic reply. The next morning Puccini delivered the autographed copy, which he had written out the night before, and received $3000 in return: not bad for writing out three pages of music! Overjoyed, Puccini rushed to Fifth Avenue and the boat was shipped out to Italy soon after.

.'Why did Puccini sue Al Jolson?' was a question asked on a radio quiz programme I heard some years ago. The answer, of course, is that Puccini *didn't* sue Al Jolson: whoever submitted the question had simply failed to do his homework. The question should have been: *Why did Puccini's publisher sue the composer of the song 'Avalon' for which Jolson had merely written the words?* This, you will agree, is something entirely different.

The facts are these. In 1921, Puccini's publisher Ricordi claimed that the opening bars of Cavaradossi's aria 'E lucevan le stelle" from *Tosca* had been plagiarised by the American composer Vincent Rose, who used them in his song *Avalon.* Listening to the song today one can find little resemblance, if any, between its opening bars and those of Cavaradossi's heartbreaking farewell to life in act 3. The court, however, thought otherwise, and Puccini was awarded the sum of $25.000.

While staying at a hotel in Milan, Puccini heard an old organ-grinder slowly churning out the melody of "Vissi d'arte'. Angered by the dragging tempo Puccini rushed out of the hotel and grabbing the handle of the organ began to play the aria. "There!" said Puccini angrily, "that's the correct tempo for my music!" and re-entered the hotel in a better frame of mind. The next day the organ-grinder was back in the street. Proudly displayed on his machine was a placard that read:

GENARRO DI PASQUALE
PUPIL OF PUCCINI

In 1920 Puccini was asked by the mayor of Rome to compose an anthem, the *Inno di Roma,* in honour of the Eternal City. It was given its first performance in Rome in the open air and was attended by the King. Although it achieved a fair success, Puccini afterwards declared it to be *una vera porcheria* (absolute trash).

A curious incident marred the performance. As the chorus of 1200 voices launched into the refrain 'Sole che sorgi libero e giocondo' ('Sun rising free and joyful') ') the words were greeted by such a torrential downpour of rain that audience, chorus and orchestra had to flee for shelter!

While Puccini was working on *La Bohème* he and his cronies clubbed together and purchased at Torre del Lago a disused inn which they promptly named *Club La Bohème.* Here, in convivial company, Puccini ate, drank, smoked, played cards and composed music. Among the club's 'regulations' were:

> *4: The Treasurer is empowered to abscond with the funds*
> *7: Silence is prohibited*

It was Puccini's custom to send his friends a *panettone* for Christmas. He did this by sending the list of friends to a baker who then delivered the *panettoni* to the addresses given. One Christmas, following a bitter row with Toscanini, Puccini forgot to take the conductor's name off the list. Angry with himself, Puccini sent Toscanini a curt telegram:

PANETTONE SENT BY MISTAKE. PUCCINI

back came the reply:

PANETTONE EATEN BY MISTAKE. TOSCANINI

Queens

What is possibly the most dramatic encounter between two characters in opera, Mary, Queen of Scots and Elizabeth I of England, occurs in act 2 of Donizetti's opera *Maria Stuarda*. The fact that this meeting never actually took place in history but only in Schiller's fertile imagination need not concern us here. Mary, goaded beyond endurance by Elizabeth's false accusations of treachery, slaps her face with her glove and replies in kind with the following words The English translation is taken from the English version of the opera):

Figlia impure di Bolena	Shameless daughter of a harlot!
parli tu del disonore?	How dare you speak of dishonour?
Meretrice indegna, oscena	You licentious, painted creature
in te cada il mio rossore	how I blush for your behaviour!
Profanato è il soglio inglese	Dishonoured is the throne of England
vil bastarda,dal tuo pié!	royal bastard, all these years!

Quiz answers on page 97-98

1. Which famous tenor created the role of Frederick Löwe and in which opera?

2. Tosca's first name is Floria; Cavaradossi's is Mario; what is Scarpia's? [clue: it's not in the opera but in the play by Sardou on which the opera is based]

3. Which opera by Puccini is based on the same story as Adam's ballet *Giselle?*

4. Mozart's *Figaro* and Rossini's *Barber* are based on two plays, part of a trilogy by the French writer Beaumarchais. What's the name of the third play and which composer set it to music?

5. Name the composer who wrote a *Barber of Seville* before Rossini.

6. Who was Tobia Gorrio?

7. Many characters in opera assume false names. In which operas do the following names occur and what are their real names?
   a. Gualtier Maldé   **b.** Idia Legray   **c.** Don Felice de Bornos   **d.** Samuel   **e.** Julia

8. Owing to censorship or other reasons some operas had their titles changed before they were allowed to be staged. Give the names of these operas as we know them today.
   a. *Il finto Stanislao*   *b*. *Nino re d'Assiria*   *c*. *Una vendetta in domino*   *d*. *Les Martyrs*
   e. *Giovanna di Guzman*   *f*. *La disfatta degli Austriaci*

9. How did these heroines meet their death?
   a. Adriana Lecouvreur   b. La Wally   c. La Gioconda   d. Norma   e. Selika

10. What was the first opera to be broadcast live and its date?

11. In which opera does Puccini quote a theme from an opera by Richard Strauss?

12. What have the composer Eugene d'Albert and King Henry VIII in common?

13. Most opera buffs know that, in private life, Adelina Patti was known as Baroness Cederström. Here are the married names of ten celebrated singers. What are their professional names?
   a. Mrs H Armstrong   **b.** Mrs K Wilson   **c.** Mrs C Rubinstein   **d.** Mrs A Samuels   **e.** Mrs K Johansen   **f.** Mrs R Jackson   **g.** Mrs L Bazelli   **h.** Mrs B. Greenough   **i.** Mrs G Tellegan   **j.** Mrs C Rumford

14. From which earlier opera did Offenbach lift the piece of music that later became the celebrated Barcarolle in *The Tales of Hoffmann?*

15. What have the actions of these three *verismo* operas in common: *Cav, Pag, Tosca?*

16. What was Susanna's 'secret' in Wolf-Ferrari's opera *Il Segreto di Susanna?*

17. In which opera would you find **a.** Polly Smith **b.** Betsy White **c.** Sally Fox?

18. Which famous 19th century Viennese music critic was parodied by Wagner in one of his operas?

19. Under what name is 'Rafaello Bartolo' better known?'

20. In 1884 an opera was produced which was so successful that the composer later wrote a sequel. Name the composer and his two operas.

Records and Recording

Opera on record has been with us for nearly 120 years. It began in 1902 when a young tenor by the name of Enrico Caruso, (q.v.) recorded ten arias from operas by Verdi, Puccini, and other composers. By doing so he brought opera into the lives – and homes - of millions of people who otherwise would have known nothing about it. By a lucky chance, the beginning of Caruso's career coincided with the advent of the gramophone, and with the issue of these ten records he, more than any other recording artist, was responsible for putting the gramophone and the recording of serious music on the world map.

A question often asked: "Did Caruso make the gramophone, or did the gramophone make Caruso?" need not concern us here but may be answered with a lukewarm *yes* to both parts.

The story of how Caruso came to make his first records forms a fascinating and unique chapter in recording history. At the age of 29, Caruso was wowing them at La Scala in the premiere of Franchetti's opera *Germania*. In the audience was Fred Gaisberg, chief recording manager of The Gramophone Company, later to become better known as His Master's Voice. Realising the tremendous potential Caruso had as a recording artist, Gaisberg offered him £100 to record ten titles, to which the tenor agreed. Gaisberg then cabled the company in London with the exciting news: back came the oft-quoted reply:

FEE EXORBITANT: FORBID YOU TO RECORD

To Gaisberg's eternal credit he decided to ignore the cable. The next afternoon Caruso sauntered into the Grand Hotel de Milan, where the recording equipment had been set up, took off his jacket, recorded the ten arias with piano accompaniment, pocketed his fee and left, all within the space of two hours. The records sold like the proverbial hot cakes and the company, thanks to Gaisberg's foresight, made a nett profit of some £15 000. As time went on the sales of his records helped to make Caruso an international celebrity, from which he was to earn nearly two million dollars in royalties and fees. The identity of the sender of the telegram, although known, has never been revealed.

Caruso's recording of 'Vesti la giubba', made in 1907, was the first **operatic 78** (HMV DB 111) to sell one million copies; this figure includes sales of his two previous recordings of the same aria, made in 1902 and 1904 respectively. The first **operatic LP** to sell one million copies (HMV ALP 1071) was Mario Lanza's *The Great Caruso*, the soundtrack of which includes 'Vesti la giubba'.

Other notable landmarks in the history of sound recording were the first electrical recordings (1925) and the first long-playing records (1948), although experiments in LP had been made as early as 1931 by RCA Victor.

Caruso's first records were single-sided discs 25cm (10in) in diameter and with a maximum playing time of three minutes; later, 30cm (12in) records were produced, increasing the playing time to four minutes. Who could have foreseen that 80 years later another disc, only 12cm (4,8 in) in diameter, containing up to 80 minutes of music and not using a needle, would become the norm.

The first complete opera to be recorded was *Ernani*, issued in 1903 on 40 single-sided discs; today, it is available with several different casts, on two CDs.

Gioacchino Rossini

This musical genius, born on 29th February 1792, was as famous for his wit as for his operas. One day he met by chance the manager of the Paris Opéra who, thinking to please him, said "Ah, cher maitre, the second act of your *Guillaume Tell* is to be given at the Opéra tonight!" Rossini, who deeply resented the way his opera (it was nearly five hours long) had been dismembered in performance, exclaimed in mock surprise: "What! the whole of it!".

Rossini and Meyerbeer both lived in Paris and the rivalry between them was legendary. One day, a group of street musicians began playing noisily outside Meyerbeer's house. Unable to concentrate on his composing Meyerbeer offered the leader 50 francs to play outside Rossini's apartment in the Chaussée d'Antin. Much embarrassed, the leader replied that *helás!* he couldn't accept: *maitre* Rossini had paid him 100 francs to play outside Meyerbeer's house!

Whenever a performance was announced of a Rossini opera it was Meyerbeer's habit to send two elegantly-dressed men to attend -not to listen but to publicly fall asleep. They became known as *Les sommeilleurs de Meyerbeer.*

When Meyerbeer died, his nephew called on Rossini and asked if he could play him a funeral dirge he had composed in honour of his illustrious uncle. When he had finished, he asked the celebrated maitre for his opinion. Taking a pinch of snuff, Rossini replied he thought it was very good but it would have been even better if the nephew had died and Meyerbeer had composed the music...

When the 19-year old Adelina Patti was in Paris she visited Rossini to pay her respects. While there she offered to sing 'Una voce poco fa,' complete with all kinds of embellishments, to Rossini's accompaniment. When she had finished, Rossini's comment was: "What a beautiful aria; who wrote it?"

The music of the celebrated Cat Duet was taken from arias in Rossini's *Otello* and arranged as a duet by the Belgian composer Berthold.

Rossini, a great gourmet created many recipes. His most famous dish is *Tournedos Rossini*, consisting of a prime fillet steak garnished with strips of bacon.

Having become bald at an early age, Rossini had a collection of seven wigs of different colours which he changed every day. This way, he told a friend, he knew which day of the week it was. His sense of humour never left him.

Rossini died in Paris in 1868. His body was returned to Italy in 1887 to the church of Santa Croce in Florence, where his tomb, erected in 1912, may be seen today.

Titta Ruffo

How many opera lovers know that this great baritone was named after a dog? His father Oreste Titta, had a hunting-dog called Ruffo of which he was very fond. The dog died in 1877 and when, a few months later, Oreste's son was born he named him Ruffo in memory of the dog. When Ruffo Titta decided to embark on a singing career he inverted his name and became Titta Ruffo.

In 1903 Ruffo was at Covent Garden singing in *Lucia*. Also in the season was *Rigoletto*, but the baritone engaged for the role fell ill and Ruffo was asked to take over. During rehearsals Nellie Melba, as Gilda, realising she would be totally upstaged by Ruffo's magnificent voice, complained to the management that Ruffo was too young to be her father and refused to sing with him. Ruffo was dismissed but eight years later got his revenge. The two had been cast to sing in *Rigoletto* in Buenos Aires. By this time Ruffo, a world-famous Rigoletto, told the management he could not sing with Melba because she was too *old* to be his daughter.

Rusalka

The British premiere of Dvorak's *Rusalka* was to take place at Sadlers Wells in 1959. The title-role was to be sung by Joan Hammond, and the cast had been rehearsing for weeks. On the day of the premiere, just three hours before the curtain was to go up, she received an urgent telephone call from the manager. Tenor Charles Craig had lost his voice: could she sing Butterfly instead? Although she hadn't sung the part for months, she agreed, and on the train journey to London took the score and mentally went through the role until she felt confident. Hollywood couldn't have done it better.

On arriving at the stage door she was greeted by the stage manager with the words: "Joan, we're doing *Rusalka* after all! Charles Craig has decided to go through with it!" The mental switch from Puccini to Dvorak in a few minutes was an astonishing feat of willpower but she succeeded and the premiere was a great success. Her recording of 'O silver moon', which had seldom been recorded before, also helped to make the opera popular.

S

Antonio Salieri

Is there a more maligned composer in the history of opera than Antonio Salieri? One of the most respected musicians of his generation, Salieri composed 39 operas, 11 cantatas and six masses. As a teacher he could boast among his pupils Beethoven, Schubert and Liszt. He was appointed Court Composer by Emperor Joseph II of Austria and in 1778 enjoyed international fame when his opera, *Europa riconosciuta,* was chosen to inaugurate the newly-built Teatro alla Scala in Milan. Yet this is the man who stands accused of having poisoned Mozart.

How did this mischief start? It seems that immediately following Mozart's death in 1791, malicious rumours began circulating that he had been poisoned by Salieri. While Salieri may have been jealous of his younger rival that doesn't mean he poisoned him. Then, about 40 years later, the Russian poet Alexander Pushkin wrote a short play, *Mozart and Salieri,* in which Salieri, after inviting Mozart to an inn, offers him a glass of poisoned wine. The unsuspecting Mozart drinks it, but soon after feels unwell, goes to lie down and dies.

The myth was next perpetuated by Nicolaii Rimsky-Korsakov, who set Pushkin's play to music. Also titled *Mozart and Salieri,* the opera was produced in Moscow in 1898, with the great Russian bass Feodor Chaliapin as Salieri. As in the play, Salieri invites Mozart to an inn where he poisons his wine. Mozart dies soon after.

About 100 years later the story was given another twist when Peter Schaffer's stage play *Amadeus,* and later film, were produced. Both play and film open with a scene in which Salieri publicly declares

"Mozart! Forgive your assassin! I confess: I killed you!"

The fact that Mozart died of acute nephritis was ignored in turn by poet, composer and playwright: death by poisoning is, after all, far more spectacular, especially on stage, than dying from inflammation of the kidneys. Despite Salieri's innocence, there still lurks the suspicion, at least in the popular mind, that he poisoned Mozart. Don Basilio, in his aria 'La calunnia è un venticello' from *The Barber,* was spot on when he describes how slander can grow from a gentle breeze into a gale of such force that a person's reputation is easily destroyed. *Povero Salieri!*

Tito Schipa

Soon after WW2 famous Italian tenor Tito Schipa went on a concert tour of Jugoslavia. On his return to Italy a friend asked how it went. Schipa replied that it went very well: every town he visited had posters and banners proclaiming, in giant letters,

VIVA TITO!

He was, Schipa told his friend, tongue in cheek, most gratified by these manifestations of enthusiasm for a visiting tenor.

The following is from Tito Gobbi's *My Life* and is reproduced by kind permission of the publishers, Macdonalds & Janes, London.

During a performance of *The Barber of Seville* with Schipa, Gobbi received a tremendous ovation after 'Largo al factotum', the applause continuing for a long time. However, when the performance resumed he found he was in some kind of vocal trouble: he had difficulty reaching his lower notes and found it very hard to produce the right tones the role required. During the interval he told Schipa about his problem, who suddenly became somewhat embarrassed.

"I'm sorry, Tito," he said, "I should have told you. You see, sometimes I have trouble with those high notes in the scene following your aria, so the orchestra transposes the music down. We keep up the applause so that the audience won't notice the change in key!" So much, thought Gobbi, for *his* 'ovation'!

After a performance of *Martha* in Chicago Schipa and his wife left the theatre and entered a nearby pharmacy to buy some medicine for their little daughter. At the entrance he was stopped by a beautiful young girl who asked "Excuse me, but aren't you Tito Schipa?" "Yes," replied Schipa. "Oh my darling angel!" exclaimed the girl, and before Schipa knew what was happening she had planted a resounding kiss on his lips.

"Who is that woman?" asked his wife, to which Schipa replied that he had never seen her before. At this the girl went pale, dropped to her knees and amid sobs said to his wife: "Oh please forgive me! I kissed your husband because tonight he sang so divinely. But the kiss was for the artist, not the man!" Um, how exactly do you distinguish between a kiss intended for Lionello and not for Schipa?

Leo Slezak

As a young unknown singer, Slezak qualified to receive free tickets to performances at Bayreuth, on condition that he audition for Frau Wagner afterwards. The day of the audition came and he was ushered into the presence of the great Cosima herself. When asked what he was going to sing Slezak replied 'Vesti la giubba' from *I Pagliacci*.

The stunned silence that greeted his announcement was only broken by the astonished gasp of the musical director. After Frau Wagner had recovered from the shock she rather coldly suggested he should sing something by the *Meister*. Accordingly, Slezak chose an aria from *Das Rheingold* but lying somewhat in the lower register he sang it very badly and was dismissed with

78

the remark that his vocal technique was still rather scanty. The story did the rounds for years and whenever Slezak's name cropped up, people used to say "Ah, yes; he's the fellow who tried to sing *Pagliacci* at Bayreuth!".

While touring in the United States Slezak arrived in Colorado, where he sang Samson. The next day he found, much to his astonishment, the theatre closed: the tour manager had absconded with the takings, the cast had not been paid and the sheriff had attached the theatre's assets, including Slezak's own costumes. In a towering rage –and Slezak towered six feet six inches in height – he pushed aside the six policemen guarding the sheriff's office, burst open the door and confronted the sheriff's men. He explained that he was leaving Colorado tomorrow for Europe and that he needed his costumes for his next appearance, which was scheduled to take place in Russia.

Impressed by his determination and no doubt his build they released the costumes and early the next morning he drove to the station to catch the Chicago express bound for New York. On the front page of a local newspaper he read the headline

GIANT CZECH TENOR WHIPS SIX POLICEMEN!

Oscar Straus

Although it's hardly surprising that Oscar Straus's surname would be confused with that of the more famous Strauss, you would think the Town Council of Bad Ischl in the Salzkammergut where Straus resided would get it right, but it was not to be.

In honour of its celebrated fellow-citizen, the Town Council had decided to rename a stretch of road alongside the river Traun 'Oscar Straus Quay'. Amid crowds of invited guests the mayor delivered his speech, an orchestra played a fanfare and Straus was given the honour of unveiling the historic plaque. His reaction has not been recorded but the plaque read:

OSKAR STRAUSS-QUAY

Francesco Tamagno

Francesco Tamagno, creator of Otello, enjoyed two reputations: one as opera's most powerful tenor, the other as opera's most stingy singer.

Having been engaged by the Met to sing Otello, Tamagno was given a first-class ticket to travel to New York by ship. Also on board was Maurice Grau, the Met's manager. After some time Grau noticed that Tamagno was missing and, fearing the worst, immediately organised a search. The missing tenor was found, safe and well, holed up in second-class: he had quietly traded in his first-class ticket for a second-class and pocketed the difference.

On another occasion Tamagno had been invited with other guests by the conductor Mancinelli to a luncheon at Milan's famed Cova restaurant. On the menu was *cotoletta alla milanese*. After the guests had been served Tamagno, noticing some cutlets were left untouched, leaned over and asked Mancinelli what he would do with them. "Do with them?" replied the astonished conductor, "Nothing!" "In that case", said Tamagno, "I'd like them for my little dog; he loves *cotolette alla milanese*", and calling a waiter, had them wrapped up to take away.

The following day Mancinelli had to visit Tamagno at his apartment in Milan. He found the tenor and his daughter at lunch tucking into an appetising dish of guess what?...*cotolette alla milanese!* And so the poor doggy had none…

Richard Tauber singer, conductor, composer.

Singer

Born in Linz, upper Austria in 1891, son of a Catholic mother and a Jewish father, Tauber inherited his musical and dramatic gifts from his parents at an early age. His mother was a soubrette who sang first in Vienna and then in provincial opera houses; his father was an actor who later became manager of the Chemnitz Opera House. It was here, at the age of 21, that Tauber made his debut as Tamino in *Die Zauberflöte*, the first step in a career that was to make him the foremost Mozart tenor of his time in Austria and Germany.

Thanks to his brilliant musicianship – he had trained as a conductor in Frankfurt - Tauber quickly became known as a tenor who could take on roles at short notice. At 23, he was summoned by Richard Strauss to sing the role of Bacchus in *Ariadne auf Naxos* in Berlin, the tenor cast for the part having fallen ill. Although he had never sung the part before he learned it in the two days preceding the opening night. After the performance Strauss, who was conducting, thanked him and remarked how lucky it was that he had sung the role before. When Tauber replied that tonight was the first time, Strauss was so angry that he told the tenor that had he known he would never have conducted the opera!

In July 1926, Dresden scored a coup: it had obtained the exclusive rights to premiere Puccini's *Turandot* in Germany, within a few weeks of the world premiere at La Scala. Once again, the tenor engaged for the part of Calaf had taken ill and Tauber, who was now part of the Dresden company, was asked to take over at three days' notice. Never a 'top-note' tenor, Tauber nevertheless sang the role of the Unknown Prince extremely well and his performance was praised by the critics.

It was at about this time that Tauber met Franz Lehár. A partnership was forged resulting in Lehár composing some of his greatest works: *Paganini, Der Zarevitch, Friederike, The Land of Smiles* and *Giuditta* (qv), with Tauber as leading tenor. The highlight in all these works was the

'Tauberlied', a hit song composed by Lehár to show off the tenor's voice: in *The Land of Smiles* it was 'Dein ist mein ganzes Herz' ('You are my heart's delight'). It became Tauber's signature tune and according to one estimate he sang it over 7 000 times!

An amusing incident took place on Tauber's first visit to London: he had been engaged to sing in the first English production of *The Land of Smiles* at Drury Lane. As his train from Dover pulled into Victoria Station he found hundreds of people waiting on the platform to greet him. As he stepped out of the carriage a spontaneous cheer went up. Delighted with his reception, he waved to the crowd in appreciation. What he didn't know was that travelling on the same train was King Alfonso of Spain, who had abdicated the day before: the crowd had come to greet *him!*

During his stay in London, Tauber met the English actress Diana Napier, whom he married four years later. He was then appearing at the Salzburg Festival, and wanting to show his bride-to-be the delights of Germany, they decided to drive to Munich for lunch. As they took their places at a table in the famous Walter Spiel restaurant, Diana noticed the unfriendly looks directed at them. The waiter slammed their food down on the table and hostile comments were made. Suddenly, an enormously stout man approached their table and told Diana to get her future husband out of Germany as quickly as possible. As they hurried back to their car she asked who the man was. "Hermann Goering," replied Tauber grimly, "he is one of my greatest fans and has all my records". Later they discovered that the restaurant was a regular hangout for Nazi bigwigs from Berlin and elsewhere.

Conductor

Tauber's fame as a conductor can be said to have begun in wartime Britain. Owing to the absence of opera in England during WW2 he turned to conducting, especially the London Philharmonic Orchestra (LPO) which he took on tours throughout the country, thus proving his worth as a first-rate orchestral conductor. Nor was there anything gimmicky about his conducting. The concerts were reviewed by the critics in much the same way as those conducted by Beecham, Boult, Sargent and other British conductors of the time. In addition to symphonies by Mozart, Schubert, Beethoven and other composers, he conducted performances of stage works such as *Gay Rosalinda,* adapted from *Die Fledermaus, The Bird Seller* and others.

Composer

As a composer of operettas and musical shows, Tauber displayed another facet of his musical gifts. Among his various works for stage and screen were *Old Chelsea, The Singing Dream, Heart's Desire* and *Franz im Glück.* He also composed a symphonic piece, The *Sunshine Suite,* inspired by his visit to South Africa, which he later conducted for a recording.

Tauber's career ended in the same way as it had begun, with Mozart. In 1947 the Vienna Opera and Philharmonic Orchestra had been invited to Covent Garden to give performances of several operas, among them *Don Giovanni.* Tauber, by now seriously ill with lung cancer, was invited to sing Don Ottavio with his former colleagues from Vienna. And so on the night of 27 September, refusing any fee and singing on one lung, he gave one of the finest performances of his life. As events turned out, it was his last. The next day he entered hospital where cancer of the other lung was diagnosed. A period of convalescence followed but he failed to recover and in January 1948 died at the age of 56. A requiem mass was held at the Catholic Church in Spanish Place in central London in his memory.

Recordings

During his lifetime Tauber made over 700 recordings, comprising opera, operetta, oratorio, Lieder, folksongs and songs from musicals of the day such as *Oklahoma!* To the latter he gave the same care and attention as he gave to the songs of Mozart, Schubert and Schumann. Not until very late in his career did he agree to accept royalties from his records. This was because he was always short of money and records provided a handy source of income. Paradoxically, the man who thrilled millions with his voice and who spent hundreds without a thought ended up owing the Department of Inland Revenue £22.000 in unpaid taxes; it took his widow four years to repay the debt.

Top Cs

Top C-Turvy would not be complete without a mention of that applause-catching high note so beloved of sopranos and tenors and, of course, by their audiences.

Paradoxically, opera's most famous top C, in 'Di quella pira,' was not even written by Verdi. It was inserted either by Carlo Baucardé or Enrico Tamberlick, two 19th century tenors famous for their high notes. Verdi, who normally objected to singers changing his music, in this instance seems not to have minded. "If you're going to sing a high C", he told Baucardé, "make sure it's a good one."

Many arias, of course, contain notes higher than top C. Arturo in *I Puritani* has a C sharp *in alt* in his first act romanza, while later in the opera he has a high F to contend with, written by Bellini for Rubini, the first Arturo. This note is usually omitted since few tenors can reach it.

Other famous high notes are Raoul's top D flat at the end of the final duet in *Les Huguenots*; Elvira's E flat at the close of the *Puritani* Mad Scene; Chapelou's top D in *Le Postillon de Longjumeau*; the Queen of the Night's top Fs in *Die Zauberflöte;* and Lady Macbeth's high D flat that closes her Sleepwalking Scene. But the aria that 'tops' them all is Tonio's cabaletta in *La fille du regiment:* not one top C but nine! You can hear them on recordings made by, *inter alia*, Benvenuto Finelli, Luciano Pavarotti, Deon van der Walt and Rockwell Blake.

Tosca

It's not generally known that there might have been two *Toscas*. Alberto Franchetti, a contemporary of Puccini, had signed an agreement with Ricordi as early as 1893 giving him exclusive rights to Sardou's play. But because Puccini also wanted to compose an opera on the subject a plot was hatched to dissuade Franchetti from composing it. The double-dealing that ensued was worthy of Scarpia himself.

At a meeting between Franchetti, Ricordi and Illica, the librettist, Ricordi told the gullible Franchetti that, in his opinion, *Tosca* was too violent a subject for an opera. What with two murders, two suicides, a torture scene and an attempted rape, it could only lead to failure and Franchetti's reputation would suffer as a result. The ploy worked. The grateful Franchetti gave up his composing rights; the next day Puccini signed a contract with Ricordi to compose an opera called *Tosca!*

The premiere in 1900 in Rome was conducted by the fiery Neapolitan Leopoldo Mugnone, after which several provincial cities invited him to conduct the new opera, using local casts. In one city, the tenor cast as Cavaradossi sang so badly that as the firing-squad was lining up in act 3, Mugnone shouted out from the pit: "Soldiers! use real bullets!"

During rehearsals at the New York City Opera in 1960 the Tosca, a rather large American soprano, had so angered the backstage staff that they decided to get their revenge. In normal performances, after throwing herself off the parapet of Castel Sant'Angelo, Tosca lands on a mattress positioned a few feet below. But in this performance a trampoline had been substituted. It is said that she bounced back 15 times, in full view of the audience, who were helpless with laughter.

Arturo Toscanini

Most anecdotes about the great Italian maestro relate either to his prodigious memory or his violent behaviour on the rostrum. Of the first, perhaps the best known is when a clarinet player said that he couldn't play that evening because his E flat key had broken off. After some moments of thought Toscanini told the astonished player that he *could* play: there was no E flat in his part!

Of the second, the story goes that in a moment of uncontrollable rage during a rehearsal Toscanini took his gold watch off its chain, flung it on the ground and crushed it to pieces under his foot. The next day the orchestra duly presented him with a cheap nickel watch inscribed *For rehearsal purposes only*. However, some anecdotes show him in a kindlier light...

In 1902 at La Scala, a virtually unknown tenor by the name of Enrico Caruso (q.v) was singing Nemorino in *L'elisir d'amore*. After his 'Una furtiva lagrima' Toscanini turned to Gatti-Casazza, then La Scala's general manager and said: "By God! if this Neapolitan continues to sing like this he'll make the whole world talk about him", which is precisely what 'this Neapolitan' achieved.

During the first rehearsals of *Madama Butterfly* at the Met, Toscanini became involved - in more ways than one – with the Met's reigning prima donna, the glamorous Geraldine Farrar. "I am a star", she informed him when he carped about her tempo, 'and it's for you to follow me when I sing". "Madame", he is reputed to have replied, "the only stars I know are those in heaven".

Toscanini has also gone down in history as the only musician who openly defied fascist dictator Benito Mussolini. At public performances of operas and concerts the fascist hymn *Giovinezza* had to be played; this Toscanini absolutely refused to do. Things came to a head in 1931 when at a concert in Bologna a group of fascist thugs surrounded Toscanini's car as he arrived at the theatre. As he stepped out he was greeted with insults and then struck on the temple and upper lip, causing it to bleed. His driver immediately got him, his wife and daughter back into the car and to his hotel, which they left early the next morning. The incident provoked a furore in the international press, and Toscanini's passport, which had been confiscated, had to be returned, much to the *Duce's* embarrassment.

La traviata

As all opera-lovers know, the first night of of *La traviata* on 6 March 1853 at the Teatro La Fenice was a fiasco. "Is the fault mine or the singers" Verdi wrote to his friend Muzio. "Time will tell". Among the reasons cited is that it was performed in modern dress, as was Dumas' play *La dame aux camellias* upon which Verdi's opera is based. However, according to the Fenice's first night *cartellone,* the action takes place in about 1700, or the time of Louis XIV. This is confirmed by the review in a local newspaper the next day, which stated that *La traviata* was set around 1700. So why put it back 150 years? It's believed that the Fenice management, wary of staging an opera in modern dress and with a courtesan as heroine, decided to play safe and put the action back to the early 18th century.

Another reason for the first-night fiasco put the blame on the singers, especially Fanny Salvini-Donatelli, a soprano as double-barrelled as her name. The sight of this extremely buxom lady dying of consumption in the last act proved too much for the first-night audience, who burst out laughing. Recent research however claims that *La traviata* was not such a failure as previously reported: it was given nine times during the season and attracted good box office receipts.

Violetta was based on Dumas' heroine Marguerite Gauthier, who in turn was based on the real-life Marie du Plessis, the most celebrated courtesan in Paris. Tall and slender, with black hair and a pink and white complexion, her beauty was legendary. According to people who knew her she could hold an intelligent conversation on most subjects and a well-known critic on Paris society wrote that she could have passed as a duchess. Dumas himself said that "her lips were red as cherries and her teeth the most beautiful in the world". Marie du Plessis achieved immortality by dying of consumption at the early age of 23.

Turandot

Of those operas that were left unfinished, Puccini's *Turandot* is undoubtedly the most celebrated. Having died from a heart attack in 1924 while being treated for throat cancer – Puccini was an inveterate smoker – the task of completing it was entrusted to Franco Alfano. Working from Puccini's 36 pages of sketches, Alfano produced a convenient, if not wholly satisfying, ending, and this is the version usually performed today. Another ending, composed by Luciano Berio, was first given in London in 2003.

Puccini's opera is based on the 18th century play by Carlo Gozzi; the little slave-girl Liù is entirely the creation of Puccini's librettists, Simoni and Adami. In the play, the answers to Turandot's three riddles are Sun, Year and the Lion of the Adria (Venice). But Puccini, dissatisfied with Gozzi's somewhat nondescript riddles, instructed his librettists to create more difficult ones, in keeping with Turandot's cruel nature, hence the answers became Hope, Blood and Turandot.

Nicola Vaccai

Although best known as a singing teacher - his *Metodo pratico di canto italiano* is still in use today - Vaccai composed several operas. In fact, it was the custom in 19th century Italy to substitute the last scene of his *Giulietta e Romeo* for the last scene of Bellini's *I Capuletti ed I Montecchi* (see Leslie Orrey *Bellini* Dent 1969).

Giuseppe Verdi

The greatness of *Otello* and *Falstaff* is due not only to Verdi's musical genius but to the masterly craftsmanship of Arrigo Boïto, whose two librettos are among the finest ever written. It was an exceptionally fruitful collaboration and more's the pity that it hadn't begun earlier. And there's the rub, because it could have. As a member of the *Scapigliatura Milanese*, a group of avant-garde intellectuals generally opposed to traditional Italian art, Boïto was their outspoken leader. At a banquet given in honour of one of their members Boïto, then only 21, stood up and read a poem on the decadent state of Italian music. The fourth stanza of the poem contained the following notorious line:

Forse già nacque chi sovra l'altare	Perhaps he is already born who, modest
rizzerà l'arte, verecondo e puro	and pure, will restore Art
su quell'altar bruttato come un muro	to the altar,
di lupanare	that altar stained like the wall of a brothel

Boïto's poem may have been written in the form of a Sapphic ode, but the inference fooled no one. Verdi took the remark as a personal attack on his music and for 16 years the relationship between the two was strained. It was Verdi's publisher Ricordi who brought them together and that is how *Otello* and *Falstaff* came to be written.

We began *Top C-Turvy* with a letter from signor Bertani complaining about a performance of *Aïda* in Parma in 1871; three years later, the premiere of the Verdi *Requiem* in Milan sparked off another complaint. Hans von Bülow, eminent pianist, conductor and former husband of Cosima Liszt, happened to be in Milan at the time. Although he had not heard a note of the music he published the following notice in the Italian newspapers:

> **'Hans von Bülow was not present at the show given yesterday at the church of San Marco. Hans von Bülow must not be included among those foreigners in Milan who came to hear Verdi's sacred music.'**

And in the *Allgemeine Musikalische Zeitung* he wrote this offensive notice:

> **'Verdi, the omnipotent corruptor of artistic taste in Italy, hopes to sweep away the last remains of Rossini's immortality which he finds inconvenient. His latest opera, in ecclesiastical garb, will be exposed, after the first fictitious compliment to the memory of the poet, for three evenings to the world's admiration, after which it will be accompanied by the trained soloists to Paris, the aesthetic Rome of the Italians'.**

For 'trained' Bülow employed the derogatory term *dressiert,* which is used for the training of circus animals. But his was a lone voice. Brahms, after examining the score, declared, "Bülow has made an ass of himself: this is the work of a genius". Eighteen years later a repentant Bülow apologised to Verdi.

In 1854 Verdi was invited to compose a grand opera for Paris, *Les Vêpres Siciliennes.* During rehearsals the soprano Sofia Cruvelli, suddenly disappeared; two weeks later there was still no sign of the missing diva. Her disappearance made headline news and a burlesque *Where's Cruvelli?* was staged in London.

Then just as suddenly as she had disappeared she returned. It transpired that she had gone on what the press called a 'trial honeymoon' with her lover, a baron Vigier and had written a letter to the management explaining her absence. This she had entrusted to her maid, who had forgotten to deliver it. Rehearsals resumed and at the premiere in June 1855 Cruvelli scored a great success. She had now become baroness Vigier and retired from the stage a year later. The 'trial honeymoon', it seems, was a success .Viva Vigier....

Theodor Wachtel

This 19th century German tenor (1823-1893) holds the world record for singing the highest number of performances of a single role: Chapelou in Adam's *Le postillon de Longjumeau*. According to Gustave Kobbé (*q.v.*) who heard him in New York in 1875, he sang it over 1200 times.

World's Greatest Tenor

Who was the World's Greatest Tenor? Although there will never be agreement on such a contentious issue – there are nearly 20 claimants to the title – general agreement among opera buffs and lovers of singing is still Caruso. Even today, nearly 100 years after his death, his records bear testimony to his unique voice.

If there are nearly 20 claimants, you may ask, how can they all be the World's Greatest Tenor? The answer is that each generation produces its own greatest tenor who, rather like the *Flavour of the Month*, is eventually replaced by the next one. Some will argue that the title is merely a catchphrase invented by concert managers and impresarios to promote whatever tenor happens to be Number One in the current Hit Parade. The appellation has been applied, *inter alia*, to Caruso, Gigli, Lazaro, McCormack, Slezak, Piccaver, Martinelli, Lauri-Volpi, Fleta, Björling, Cortis, di Stefano, Tucker, Lanza, Corelli, Domingo, Pavarotti and Kaufmann.

Gigli, a legitimate claimant if ever there was one, recalls in his memoirs opening a New York daily to be confronted by two announcements on the same page:

Gigli, the world's greatest tenor, will sing at a benefit recital for the Italian Hospital on Sunday afternoon, February 19th

the other stated: **Martinelli, the world's greatest tenor, will sing at a benefit recital for the relief society for the Aged at the Waldorf Astoria Hotel on February 26th**

Giacomo Lauri-Volpi, an early contender, based his claim on the premise that because he was the world's highest-paid tenor (the Met had agreed to pay him ten cents more (!) than Gigli's fee of $3000) he automatically qualified for the title. When Jussi Björling appeared at the Royal Albert Hall in London posters outside proclaimed him 'The World's Greatest Tenor: at the time he probably was. And American tenor Richard Tucker, while on a concert tour of South Africa, was billed 'The World's Greatest Tenor': While the title continues to be contested, here are a few anecdotes to chuckle over.

The story goes that celebrated tenor Jan Peerce and his equally celebrated brother-in-law Richard Tucker were dining in a smart New York restaurant when a waiter approached bearing on a silver platter a sealed envelope addressed to 'The World's Greatest Tenor'. Peerce, with a great show of modesty, passed the letter to Tucker, saying "It must be for you, Richard". Tucker, with an equal show of modesty, replied, "No, it must be for you, Jan". After much to-ing and fro-ing they decided to open the letter together. It began: "Dear Jussi".

One morning McCormack met Caruso by chance in the street. "And how is the world's greatest tenor this morning?" McCormack asked in his Irish brogue. "Since when, Mac", countered Caruso, "have *you* been a baritone?"

As every opera fan knows, tenors have traditionally been the butt of jokes. The definition of a tenor, it has been said, is "someone who has resonance where his brains ought to be". The eminent German conductor Hans von Bülow declared "All tenors are a disease". Then, while many singers excel at *bel canto,* tenors excel at *can belto.* Ernest Newman, doyen of English music critics, took particular delight in describing certain tenors as 'amphoras'. As defined by the dictionary, an amphora, or Greek jug, is "a two-handled, big-bellied vessel usually of clay, with a longish or shortish neck and a mouth proportioned to the size".

At one time tenors were renowned for their lack of musicianship and flamboyant behaviour, such as introducing ostentatious cadenzas at the end of 'La donna e mobile' or interpolating applause-catching high Cs in 'Di quella pira', neither of which were written by Verdi. The German tenor has even been the subject of a poem, 'The Schmaltztenor' by M.W.Branch, quoted in Robert Rushmore's *The Singing Voice.* Here is the first verse, reproduced by kind permission of the publishers:

> O hark! 'tis the voice of the Schmalztenor!
> It swells in his bosom and hangs in the air
> Like lavender-scent in a spinster's drawer
> It oozes and percolates everywhere.
> So tenderly glutinous, soothing the brute in us
> Wholly unmutinous Schmaltztenor.

Sebastien Yradier

What has the composer of *La paloma* to do with opera? Strictly speaking, nothing, but his song *El arreglito*, sub-titled *chanson havanaise*, was adapted by Bizet for the habanera in *Carmen*. Yradier had died 10 years earlier and Bizet, believing it to be a genuine folk song, never bothered to check its source.

Die Zauberflöte

Q: if Papagena is the feminine form of Papageno, why isn't Pamina *Tamina*?

A: although no one is 100% sure, it's generally believed that a careless printer, while preparing a poster for the first performance of Mozart's opera, inserted an upper case P instead of a T. The typo was never corrected and more than two centuries later we are still saddled with what is believed to be the wrong name.

Answers to quiz

1. Enrico Caruso; *Germania*

2. Vitellio

3. *Le Villi*

4. *La Mère Coupable;* Darius Milhaud

5. Giovanni Paisiello

6. Arrigo Boïto

7. a. *Rigoletto;* Duca di Mantova b. *Andrea Chénier;* Maddalena c. *La forza del destino*; Don Carlo d. *La Juive;* Prince Leopold e. *Martha;* Nancy f.*Fra Diavolo;* Fra Diavolo

8. a. *Un Giorno di Regno* b. *Nabucco* c. *Un ballo in maschera* d. *Poliuto* e. *I Vespri Siciliani* f. *La battaglia di Legnano.*

9. a. inhales poisoned violets b. avalanche c. stabs herself d. immolation e. inhales poisonous leaf

10. *Hansel and Gretel,* broadcast live from Covent Garden by the BBC in 1923.

11. *La Rondine;* the theme is from *Salome.*

12. Each had six wives.

13. **a.**Nellie Melba **b.**Kathleen Ferrier **c.**Conchita Supervia **d.**Amelita Galli-Curci **e.**Kirsten Flagstad **f.**Rosa Ponselle **g.**Luisa Tetrazzini **h.**Beverly Sills **i.**Geraldine Farrar **j.** Dame Clara Butt

14. *Die Rheinnixen,* composed 17 years before *Hoffmann.*

15. They all take place within a period of 24 hours

16. Smoking cigarettes

17. *Martha*. Three peasant girls who offer themselves for domestic hire at Richmond Market.

18. Eduard Hanslick, known in his time for his dislike of modern music. Beckmesser, the town clerk in *Die Meistersinger*, is modelled on him.

19. Figaro

20. Massenet: *Manon* and *Le Portrait de Manon*

Acknowledgements

The author gratefully acknowledges the following sources for permission to quote material used in this book:

Atkins & Newman: Beecham Stories. Futura Publications London 1978

Bing R: 5000 Nights at the Opera. Hamish Hamilton London 1972

Carner M: Puccini: A Critical Biography. Duckworth London 1958

Caruso Jnr & Farkas: Enrico Caruso, my father and my family. Amadeus Oregon 1990

Castle C & Napier Tauber: This was Richard Tauber. WH Allen London 1971

Christiansen R: Prima Donna: a history. Penguin Books Harmondsworth 1986

Curtiss M: Bizet and his World. Secker & Warburg London 1959

Douglas N: Legendary Voices. André Deutsch London 1992

Franklin D. Basso Cantante.Duckworth London 1969

Gaisberg FW Music on Record. Robert Hale London 1947

Gigli B: The Memoirs of Beniamino Gigli. Cassell London 1957

Gobbi T: My Life. Macdonalds & Jane's London 1979

Grun B: Prince of Vienna: Oscar Straus. WH Allen London 1955

Hammond J: A Voice, a Life. Gollancz London 1970

Hughes S: Famous Verdi Operas. Robert Hale London 1968

Hurok S & Goode R: Impresario. MacDonald London 1947

Levy A: Bluebird of Happiness: Memoirs of Jan Peerce. Harper & Row New York 1976

McCormack L. I hear you calling me. WH Allen London 1948

Marek G: A Front Seat at the Opera. Harrap London 1951

Martin G. The Opera Companion. MacMillan London 1962

Meneghini GB: My Wife Maria Callas. Bodley Head London 1980

Newton I. At the Piano. Hamish Hamilton London 1966

Rushmore R. The Singing Voice. Hamish Hamilton London 1971

Vickers H: Great Operatic Disasters. MacMillan London 1979

Wechsberg J. Looking for a Bluebird. Penguin Books Harmondsworth 1948

About the Author

Gerry Zwirn was born in the UK but spent much of his adult life in Italy, where he worked as a journalist, writer and technical translator. During this period he was a member of the Foreign Press Club in Rome and covered assignments for British and American publications. He then emigrated to South Africa where, among other activities, he founded the Johannesburg-based Bel Canto Club and was a guest speaker on Classic fm radio. He has lectured at the music departments of various universities, including Rhodes, Cape Town and Johannesburg, on subjects ranging from the operas of Verdi to the great singers of the past. He is a member of the American Institute for Verdi Studies based in New York.

His previous book on opera, titled Stranded Stories from the Operas, was published about nine years ago. He is married and now resides in the UK, thus completing the cycle begun over 60 years ago